Freshwater Saga

Only those who have had the experience can know what a
sense of physical and spiritual excitement comes to one
who turns his face away from men towards the unknown.
In his small way he is doing what the great explorers
have done before him, and his elation recaptures theirs.

A.R.M. Lower, *Unconventional Voyages*

FRONT COVER

Feeling a way through fog at the base of Cape Isacor, Lake Superior

ERIC W. MORSE

Freshwater Saga

Memoirs of a Lifetime
of Wilderness Canoeing
in Canada

with a foreword by
ANGUS C. SCOTT

NorthWord Inc.

Ashland, Wisconsin

Originally published in Canada in 1987 by University of Toronto Press. First published in the United States in 1987 by NorthWord Inc.

ISBN 0-942802-55-1

TO PAM

who was my bowman for most of the canoeing,

who, when I could no longer read a map without glasses,
became also my navigator,

and without whom this book would not
have been produced

Contents

Foreword

Thomas Carlyle, the nineteenth century historian and philosopher, said, 'A well-written life is almost as rare as a well-spent one.' Eric Morse writes with vigour and imagination about a life which combined recreation with historical research, a life of strenuous adventure on the rivers of northern Canada, a life that has been an inspiration to many.

Much of *Freshwater Saga* tells about his long canoe trips and it is perhaps curious that he started these rather late in life. He was forty-nine when he made his first trip on the Voyageurs highway, fifty-eight on his first trip in the Barrens, and seventy-two on his last. The book was not begun until after the author's eightieth birthday and he died before it went to press. While *Freshwater Saga* is autobiographical, it focuses attention on one aspect of his life, wilderness travel in the Arctic and sub-Arctic. Even as Eric Morse followed in the footsteps of Hearne, Franklin, Back, and the Tyrrell brothers, so this sampling of journeys on northern rivers follows in the tradition of their great sagas about Canada's northern wilderness.

Freshwater Saga captures the joy of a still morning in the Barrens, the fresh northern air scented by a blanket of delicate flowers and shrubs covering the rugged, rolling hills. Captured also are the thrill of whitewater canoeing, the camaraderie of the campsite in the evening, the frustrations when pinned down by a northern blow, the cold of the wind and the rain, the solitude, and the sense of vastness of what Sigurd Olson called 'the lonely land.' Largely anecdotal in nature, it provides a wealth of detail helpful to wilderness canoeists, and it is also informative about the history of the North, its geography, and its wildlife. It looks at northern Canada from the point of view of the recreational canoeist – which is quite different from that of a government official, an oil company executive, or a resident of Denendeh or Nunavut.

It was not until he had begun his trips in the Barrens that I came to know Eric, but through them I came to know him well. In the sixties and early seventies I spent five summer holidays with him in the Barrens. I also accompanied him on many shorter trips closer to home on such rivers as the Petawawa and the French. There, he was more relaxed than in the Barrens, and enjoyed to the full simply being on the water in a canoe on a bright summer's day.

Canoeing with Eric Morse in the North was not a leisurely holiday. It was demanding, yet at the end of the trip one felt immensely restored, as one should at the end of a holiday. The day's work was taken seriously, yet each day brought a variety of adventures. Furthermore, living in close company with Eric for a number of weeks was always instructive. Most of all, canoeing with him was fun.

Canoe trips in the Barrens are by nature demanding. The weather is uncertain and often severe. The land yields little in the way of sustenance although the rivers and lakes teem with fish. In an emergency, without radios, one is dependent for help on the chance of a passing aircraft – hardly a reliable back-up.

Eric Morse coped with the demands of the North first by meticulous and comprehensive planning. The land formations were studied. The number of feet a river dropped per mile was noted. Water levels were obtained. Aerial photographs were examined for clues for whitewater navigation and for the best portage routes. Wherever possible, reports were obtained from others who had travelled the route before, some of which went back more than one hundred and fifty years, the journals of Hearne and Franklin for instance. Pamela looked after the planning and supplying of the food. She saw to it that the menus were devised day by day with an eye to the high-energy requirements of trips in northern latitudes and such other considerations as a reasonable balance in the diet, the weight factor, and the likes and dislikes of the crew. Pamela well understood that, if an army marches on its stomach, canoeists paddle on theirs. The food was divided equally between canoes so that there would be a fair division of weight and as insurance against loss or water damage in a rapid. Equipment had to stand the rigours of a northern trip. Canoes, paddles, axes, tents, packs, and particularly clothing were all carefully scrutinized. Eric's blind spot was the medical kit which he left to a rank amateur. He considered that most medical requirements could be met by a band-aid and fortunately he was usually right.

He also coped with the demands of the North by careful day-by-day planning. He strongly believed in schedules. If twenty days were set aside for a four-hundred-mile trip, an average of twenty miles had to be covered each day. Fewer miles were scheduled for whitewater days and portaging days, but these miles had to be made up when the going was easier. High winds often pinned one down in the Barrens, and time was set aside in the schedule for this eventuality. Rising time was often 4 am or earlier in order to take advantage of good weather or to make up time. Eric was always the first up and would go from tent to tent with a weather report, usually more favourable than reality. During breakfast, which was always cooked to warm us and to give us a good start in the day, Eric would provide us with periodic reminders that we had to be on the water and ready to go in an hour and a half. The day's goal was set the night before and every day we worked to that goal. Fishing he considered a waste of time. Side trips were only possible if we were ahead of schedule; very seldom were we so fortunate.

If this sounds rather dull and too much like a military campaign, it must be remembered that we were entirely on our own and therefore it was important to stick to the schedule in order to reach our destination. The result of all this careful planning was that tripping with Eric Morse was as comfortable as could be expected in those regions. And it was safe.

Tripping with him certainly was not dull. The challenge of the North looked after that. Every day brought adventure. The country we were passing through brought a variety of delights, and Eric Morse had a variety of interests which he enjoyed sharing with others. *Freshwater Saga* reveals the depth and extent of his experience of canoeing and of travel in the Barrens. His knowledge of the fur traders who inherited the canoe from the Indians, the original Canadian canoeists, is well documented in his earlier book *Fur Trade Routes of Canada / Then and Now*. How he enjoyed talking about these early canoeing people over the ritual daiquiri before dinner at the end of a long day! Some of his concerns, his likes and dislikes, and his sense of humour would come out then. He would often reminisce about the many interesting people he had met during his time in Ottawa which spanned a period of over thirty years.

During the day he would stop to observe a flower or small plant and he came to know many of the wild flowers and plants that covered the Barrens. Although not an ornithologist, he knew quite a lot about birds and could usually identify a species quickly. He knew the ways of the animals that inhabit the Barrens. With any change in the geological formation he would compare the two and usually say something about the origins of each. He was a fountain of knowledge for those fortunate enough to travel with him.

That he wished to share his knowledge is the origin of this book. Indeed, he was by nature a teacher. His father taught for many years at Trinity College School and he himself followed in his father's footsteps. Teaching was a component of his work at the UN and with the Canadian Clubs. It was the teacher in him that motivated him to seek others younger than he to accompany him and Pamela on the long trips in the Northwest Territories. When given an LLD by Queen's University, his citation read in part, 'He taught a whole generation of Canadians the importance of recovering our heritage and using it wisely.'

On another plane, I saw Eric Morse as a rare combination of stoic and romantic. The stoic part was perseverance, determination, courage, and the drive to forge ahead under adverse conditions of climate and terrain. On the romantic side was that sense of adventure that led him to the Barrens and led him to explore the canoe routes of the fur traders, to explore the northern rivers in the days before they were much paddled for recreation; and it was a sense of adventure which enabled him to enjoy the thrill of whitewater, the challenge of discovery and the peace of a sun-filled morning on a still lake under a blue sky, miles, many hundreds of miles, from the nearest road or railway.

Freshwater Saga is the work of a man who had a deep love for the land of Canada, a love fulfilled through recreational canoeing. This book makes us aware, perhaps more keenly than before, of the heritage that has been given to us, a heritage that is to be enjoyed, not destroyed.

ANGUS C. SCOTT
Headmaster Emeritus of Trinity College School
Executive Director, Canadian Parks and Wilderness Society

Acknowledgements

Eric was unable to see this book through its final stages: the maps and illustrations were still to be done or selected. Consequently I must take responsibility for any errors and omissions in these, and for any other mistakes that I may have let slip through the editing. Eric was a perfectionist, and I cannot hope to come up to his standards.

There are many people whom he would have wished to thank, especially those who accompanied him on his canoeing through the years. He did not choose to travel alone, and the good companionship of those friends was integral to his life and to this book.

He would, I know, have wished particularly to thank those who encouraged him to write these memoirs and who were kind enough to read and comment on them in draft: Ned Franks, Bert and Mary Hamilton, and especially Ian Montagnes, who radiated an interest even from the opposite end of the earth. When Eric died, they extended their help and encouragement to me, though they are in no way responsible for any faults there may be. I am grateful to them not only for their constructive help but also for having stimulated Eric into attempting this book. A stroke in 1981 had made him give up the idea, and writing no longer came easily; moreover he did not relish writing about himself. But the challenge, to which he was prodded by these friends, proved positively therapeutic and enriched his last years. For that I cannot thank them enough.

I wish to thank R.I.K. Davidson of the University of Toronto Press for his invaluable advice and editorial help. Thanks are also due to R. Valenzuela and E. Richter for their careful work on the illustrative material. I am grateful to George Luste, Angus Scott, and Tsin Van for permission to use their photographs.

P.M.M.

Introduction

I am emboldened by the fine example of David Thompson, who in his eighties wrote his classic *Narrative* describing his experiences from 1784 to 1812. Perhaps I am also rationalizing that what an aging memory forgets and omits was forgettable. This book is intended as neither a how-to handbook nor a history of early canoeing. It is a saga, in the sense of being a personal chronicle of events over the sixty-year period 1918–78 – memoirs of a lifetime's canoeing which was almost entirely done in my vacations and for no more reason than recreation. Geographically, the book covers a good part of Canada east of the Rockies, extending north to the mainland coast of the continent; most of this canoeing was therefore on the Precambrian Shield.

The Canadian Shield was never a block to travel; in fact, it was the reverse, for the Shield helped to spin the web of interconnecting rivers and lakes that covers half of Canada, an unrivalled system of 'highways' extending over a quarter of a million square miles of forest-lakeland and comprising a good part of the whole world's fresh water. Such is the background tapestry of this tale.

E W M

Part One

HISTORIC ROUTES

An account of what led me to retrace them by canoe,
and where they led me.

Beginnings

Early influences

People who know of my early fascination with canoeing ask how this arose, for I was only a young immigrant, barely in my teens, when it first took hold of me. I suppose this to have been a result of the strong influence of the first two places I lived in, together with the subsequent impact of the Canadian Shield.

Far from growing up with something so very Canadian as canoeing, I lived my early years in India, on the other side of the world. I was born in Naini Tal, a hill station 8000 feet up in the Himalayas, on the flanks of Nepal. Here I early became acquainted with wilderness and its wildlife, for we had close access to high Himalayan 'jungle', a word signifying wilderness rather than impenetrability. Even for a small boy it was open enough for walking, and my father or my Indian bearer often took me there. I was enchanted by the wildlife, particularly the troupes of monkeys, and by the wealth of exotic birds, butterflies, and wild flowers. This jungle could be spectacular, for on a clear day the prospect extended a hundred miles to the everlasting snows of the higher Himalayas not far from Everest. On our annual journey from the plains to the mountains, I had sometimes the joy of going part of the way up to Naini Tal on elephant-back, when I was allowed to sit beside the mahout. I saw enough that I believed I was living in a world of magic.

This happy existence came to a sudden end when I was no more than five. My father's business was the manufacture of perfume from a beautifully scented blossom, growing wild – jasmine, as I recall – and the market was ruined when German chemists found a way to manufacture the perfume synthetically. As a result, in 1910 we left India and sailed for Canada. Abruptly my life was changed, for my father's next venture was a fruit farm near Hamilton, Ontario. Here on the Niagara Peninsula, which juts out between lakes Ontario and Erie, exists a relatively equable climate for growing fruit, so vulnerable to early frost.

The Niagara Peninsula was not without beauty, but the peak of its beauty was ephemeral, lasting for only the few days when the orchard trees were in bloom. Every tree, as far as the eye could see, had its cloud of blossoms: spell-binding, but not wilderness. The land was flat; the orchard trees were in straight rows; all roads met at right angles. The only moving water was in small creeks and rills that trickled into Lake Ontario. The animals were mainly domesticated dogs and cats, and the omnipresent farm horses.

For my mother, accustomed to having many servants to run the two households in India, the transition to life on a small Ontario farmstead must have been demanding, but she took it all in her stride and I never heard her complain. My father may have hoped that I would be able to help in the orchards, but he quickly categorized me as the worst fruit-picker he had ever met, and counted me out of his work-force. It was not until many years later that it was established that I was not lazy but simply colour-blind. Instead of fruit-picking, I was given the task of looking after the poultry. This I enjoyed enormously, for my father wisely gave me the feeling that I had full responsibility for the operation: the purchasing of supplies, the maintenance, and the marketing. He taught me how to keep the books, and I was expected to do so methodically. The only part that I quailed from was the sentence of death and its execution, for the birds became personal friends. Fortunately my mother took over at that stage.

I went away to school in 1917 at the age of twelve, and at the end of my first year received an invitation from Mr and Mrs Cecil Heaven, of Hamilton, to spend part of my vacation at their summer place in Haliburton County. I reflect on the generosity of this invitation, for the Heavens already had four sons, near my age, who were also school friends of mine.

This was my eye-opening introduction to the Precambrian Shield. My own strong preference when canoeing, and I believe it is general, is to travel in Precambrian terrain. Haliburton is almost entirely Precambrian: a great spread of lakes, set in granite and covered originally by forest.

I had never known, till I went to Haliburton, that such country existed, where one could travel for weeks going from lake to lake. Not only were its rock-bound rivers and lakes themselves scenic, but the rock inhibited both farming and settlement, and the forest everywhere hid and protected wildlife. Coming from settled Southern Ontario, which was all I knew of Canada till then, I became aware of a part of me that had lain dormant since I had left the wilderness of the Himalayan jungle.

The Heavens' summer place was on Horseshoe Lake, a broadening of the Gull River a little north of Minden. From there a whole wonderland of totally wild, beautiful country opened to the north, enabling one to paddle to Lake of Bays or Algonquin Park and still, at that date, without being overrun by other parties of canoeists. As it happened, I had been especially fortunate to have been asked to stay with a family — one of the very few in those days — who made a practice of going for long annual canoe trips, and soon after my arrival I was invited to replace an adult who had had to drop out of one of these expeditions. No more than three weeks long, this trip nevertheless had a great impact on me. The canoe held all our food and shelter, so that we were actually *living* in this beautiful forest, dotted with lake after lake. I had not till then seen such country or travelled in a vehicle which went so smoothly and silently, affording frequent encounters with wildlife.

All too soon, the visit was over. But on my return home I had no difficulty in persuading my parents to build a cottage on a Haliburton lake. We used to spend all summer there, three or four months of vacation, for my father had by now given up the fruit farm and had entered the teaching profession. My parents were as happy as I to revert temporarily to being, as it were, an early Canadian family 'pioneering' in the forest, on the shore of an attractive lake, spurning the motor car, and moving, when necessary, by water. Each day, I paddled the five miles into the nearest post office for the mail and went by canoe to a neighbouring farm for milk. We had a motor-boat, but when we went for a picnic or away for a whole day, and whenever time permitted, we chose to travel more silently, by canoe.

Undoubtedly, one of the aspects of canoeing that entranced me was the feeling of independence, the ability to make one's way through the country by unmechanized means. It appealed also to my imagination, for I had early been exposed to tales of travel through the wilds, though not so much by water. A family relative was F.C. Selous, born in England in 1851, who went to Africa at the age of nineteen and became a world-famous big-game hunter, safari leader, and naturalist. His quest for game had opened up much unexplored country in eastern and southern Africa. In those days, big-game hunting was by no means considered questionable, but I am glad that in later years he turned to preservation of wildlife rather than slaughter. I did not know until much later that between 1900 and 1906 his travels had even taken him to the Yukon and Newfoundland, where in search of caribou he had canoed such little-known rivers as the Macmillan and the Terra Nova: there is a Mount Selous between the two branches of the Macmillan, both of which he ascended. But it was his African exploits that I heard of as a boy; I never met him, and he was killed in Africa in 1917, having talked his way into an active command in his mid-sixties on the basis of his physical fitness and knowledge of the country. A more immediate boyhood hero was Jim Corbett, later author of *Man-eaters of Kumoan*, who was also born in Naini Tal, and whom I could just remember as a friend of my father's. He had

Lake Kashagawigamog, Haliburton: a view from the cottage

learned as a quite young boy to travel on his own in the jungle, and his tales of his experiences had entranced me.

By now I was able to plan my own canoe expeditions, and with various companions I would each year make longer trips, mostly through some loop of lakes that one could get to easily. To find wilderness canoeing in eastern Canada in those days, we seldom thought of going elsewhere than Haliburton, Muskoka, Timagami, or Algonquin Park. Our equipment was rudimentary. Tents in those days were heavy and cumbersome, and instead we draped the overturned canoes with mosquito netting and slept beneath, on beds of pine or spruce branches, overlain with tarpaulins. Specialized lightweight food was unavailable, and indeed we did not need it, for we could manage well enough with ordinary store goods, fish, and berries. I did, however, develop a lifelong dislike for blueberries, after being forced to subsist on them for several days when windbound towards the end of a trip, all other supplies exhausted.

A doctor introduced a threat to my happy existence, stating that I had a heart murmur and had better avoid over-exertion. Luckily my response was a stubborn attempt to prove him wrong: I took up cross-country running, and came to enjoy pushing myself physically, on the track and on the trail. Possibly this was the best treatment; more likely, the diagnosis was faulty. In any case, I was none the worse, and my way of life had perhaps been improved.

Another spur to my canoeing, around this time, was that it offered an escape from a somewhat dreary job. My father apparently gave no thought to higher education for me. I do not think that it was lack of care for me, or even lack of money, for he went to considerable expense on my sister's education. I believe it simply never occurred to him that I should need to do otherwise than he had himself. After teaching for a while in his father's private school in the Isle of Wight, he had obeyed a summons from a widowed aunt while still in his teens and gone out to India to help manage the perfume business. Perhaps misled by my boyhood success with the poultry, he saw a business career for me. So at sixteen I was out of school, a temporary master in a private school teaching boys older than myself, a situation that I do not remember finding either daunting or strange. And as soon as a position in the accounting office of Harris Abattoir (later Canada Packers) offered, my father encouraged me to take it. Methodical I might have been, but figures and finance did not interest me at all. I stuck it for three years, then set about training properly for a teaching career. Canoeing had been a true refuge in those years of office work.

These then were the early influences which set my steps on the 'path of the paddle'. At the same time, without my realizing it, the seeds were soon sown for a supporting interest, retracing the historic routes of the fur traders and explorers, which became a theme influencing my canoe travels after 1950. At school and university, my favourite subjects were biology, geography, and history. The links between all three in the opening up of Canada came to intrigue me. Trained as an historian, I became aware of the work of Harold Innis. His classic book, *The Fur Trade in Canada: An Introduction to Canadian Economic History* published in 1930, struck an immediate chord. I began to read all I could of the journals of the early fur trade, of explorers, and of other travellers by canoe or dog team, and began also to build up a library of those early journals. In the thirties and forties, it was my canoeing that complemented my reading. The point from which my reading gave theme and purpose to my canoeing came later, after 1950.

I took my MA at Queen's and then, on a scholarship, attended a summer semester of the School of International Studies at Geneva. I spent an extra year writing my Master's thesis, since I had come across more material in libraries in London and Geneva, and had the good fortune of access to Sir Robert Borden's papers in Ottawa on my return to Canada in 1935. The following year, I was invited to join the staff of my old school, Trinity College School at Port Hope, as senior history master and head of that department. I enjoyed teaching, particularly the senior boys, who liked being encouraged to think for themselves and debate historical, political, and economic issues. However, I did not plan making a career in teaching, since I soon began to realize this was a dead end, offering little advancement until one could consider a position administering some educational institution, which did not appeal to me. In the end, my dilemma was solved: in 1939, the Second World War broke out, and I joined the RCAF and was shortly posted to Air Force Headquarters in Ottawa.

This is a city that sits at the very edge of the Shield, which on the Quebec side comes right down to the Ottawa River. North of Ottawa I had access to canoe country close at hand, for the Gatineau, Coulonge, Lièvre, Rouge, and their tributary rivers all drain southwards off the Shield into the Ottawa River. In my vacations and weekends I made myself familiar with these waterways. By the time the war ended, Ottawa had become such a way of life for me – skiing in winter, canoeing in summer, and hiking on the hills in spring and fall – that I was loth to leave it.

In 1946, in common with a large number of other Canadians leaving military service at that time, I was faced with deciding on a career. Ottawa was where I wanted to be, in canoe country. A return to teaching did not attract me, and I was disinclined to enter the civil service, where someone else would make the main decisions, often on merely political grounds. Fortunately, just after being demobilized from the air force in 1946, I came to hear of a search committee looking for a national secretary for the newly formed United Nations Association in Canada. I became the organization's first national secretary. The job was first of all to organize branches in the main cities and then to stimulate public support for the new body, just born in 1945 at the San Francisco Conference to replace the impotent League of Nations. The CPR made the first part of this work easier, through their handsome donation to the association of a transcontinental railway pass, and I began my work travelling across Canada, helping to set up branches in every main city. I then returned to live in Ottawa and run the national office of the UN Association.

This led in 1946 to my appointment as national director of the Association of Canadian Clubs, again in Ottawa – a position

I held until my retirement in 1971. I had been lucky enough to find a job that was both challenging and congenial, and in Ottawa; I was co-ordinating the formation and operation of Canadian Clubs in large cities and in smaller communities, and persuading interesting personalities to speak on the Club circuit. True, I missed the long vacations of an academic appointment, but took every opportunity on weekends, and for three weeks in the summer, to get off on the water or the hills.

Incongruously, it was an Ottawa dinner-party in 1951 that led to the formation of the group of men with whom my canoeing took on a more serious pattern. After dinner, in a spirit of gentle banter, some of the Canadians were asking the diplomats present how they could possibly learn much of the true Canada on the cocktail circuit. They should experience what it was like to paddle Canadian lakes and rivers, trudge over portages, feel the spray of rapids, camp among pines, and face the insects. In the end the diplomats said, 'OK, show us.' So it was agreed that three Canadians, Omond Solandt, Blair Fraser, and I, would take three diplomats on a canoe trip. The diplomats were Tony Lovink, then Netherlands ambassador and dean of the diplomatic corps, and two first secretaries, 'Woody' Woodward (South Africa) and Freddy vas Nunes (Netherlands).

I was commissioned to pick a route and to lay on canoes, food, and equipment. It was an attractive, if undemanding, course that we chose, and took little more than a week – an old Indian route that descended the Gatineau River from Maniwaki, then through Thirty-one Mile Lake and Lac Pemichangan it wended its way over to the Lièvre, and finally back to the Gatineau again. Though none of the non-Canadians had ever paddled before, the trip was voted a great success, and around the last campfire the question was 'Where do we go next year?' Thus was born an informal, congenial, and strong wilderness canoeing group that has endured over the years. The press dubbed us the Voyageurs, and the name stuck. The summer trips became longer, the personnel changed from year to year as members came and went, but the association has been lasting. And as population pressures began to threaten the wilderness

Setting out on the 1952 trip that gave rise to the Voyageurs group. Left to right: 'Woody' Woodward, EWM, Omond Solandt, Freddy vas Nunes, Blair Fraser, and (inset) Tony Lovink (Photo Tsin Van, Ottawa)

in eastern canoe country, we headed west and north, to paddle some of the great rivers that had contributed to Canadian history in the days of early exploration and the fur trade.

Quetico

West we went next year, for we were hearing of the gorgeous canoe country to be found in Quetico Park lying just west of Lake Superior and north of the US border. We made three trips into this canoeing paradise, the first in 1952, when we entered Quetico Park by its northern entrance at Atikokan. That year we did no more than the standard circumnavigation of Hunter 'Island' (actually a large peninsula). In 1953 we were led by Sigurd Olson, who knew the Quetico as well as anyone, into its interior, less travelled lakes, earning our privacy by a few long or rough portages. Sig, an author and president of the American National Parks Association, then joined our group and, as he was the oldest and most experienced canoeist among us, he became our 'bourgeois' or leader. A true outdoorsman, who had served as a guide in his student days, he was becoming renowned as a perceptive wilderness writer and conservationist.

Another, earlier, addition to our party was Maj.-Gen. Elliot Rodger, shortly to become Vice Chief of General Staff of the Canadian Army. He had canoed before and delighted in running white water, his astonishing laugh sounding above the roar of rapids, especially at the most critical spots. One of the most unselfish men I have known, he was the first to see what had to be done next, and to get on and do it.

Blair Fraser, the Ottawa editor of *Maclean's* magazine and a popular broadcaster on international affairs, was a founder-member of our group, having been one of the three Canadians on our first trip in 1951. However, he was not free to join us again until 1953. He was good company, and had a fine singing voice, with a wide repertoire ranging from the ribald to the religious. His was a tragic loss when he drowned in a rapid on the Petawawa River in 1968.

Blair was one person on whom I could usually count for company during the year, either for skiing or for canoeing. Many a time we would dash off to the Laurentians in winter, driving back through the night so as to reach the office on Monday. We would keep awake by singing, choosing songs with many verses – French, French-Canadian, British – finally settling for hymns and feeling grateful that our good Christian upbringing could be put to such practical purpose. On weekends we would often take the ski-bus to Camp Fortune, the main ski-development in the Ottawa area at that time. When the snows melted, we would get in some early canoeing practice, and (more importantly) portaging practice, using the waterways of the Gatineau valley for our training-ground. It became a tradition with us to make a round of lakes and portages that included a certain fiendish Mountain Portage, where one of us would carry the canoe up the steep slope while the other carried a large pack filled with copies of the *Canada Year Book*. Our fellow-Voyageurs might scoff, but it was our turn to laugh when we started on the main summer trip, for our training certainly paid dividends.

For our third trip in Quetico, in 1954, we decided to enter by its front door, Grand Portage, and camped on the shore of Lake Superior near the mouth of the Pigeon River. We knew from Alexander Mackenzie's and other early journals that the Montreal fur traders headed west around Lake Superior's North Shore and that, when they reached the Grand Portage, they followed it up to the plateau where the continental divide lay and whence the waters flowed westward. On the way up the nine-mile portage next morning we came upon a large sign erected by the Minnesota Historical Society. This sign, which had a tremendous impact on us, informed us that the path we stood on, circumventing the unnavigable cataracts and canyons of the lower Pigeon, had first been trodden by La Vérendrye in 1732. Soon after that time it had become the way by which the voyageurs of the North West Company surmounted the plateau west of Lake Superior, 1000 feet above the lake, carrying westward the trade goods and bringing back the beaver pelts from the Athabasca country. The sign made clear, too, that

On the route through the Boundary lakes from Lake Superior
to Fort Frances:
above On the Grand Portage;
below Wading up the Pigeon River

Mackenzie, Fraser, Thompson, and other explorers of the west had used this very path. The words of the sign and the path itself were inspiring. We were for the first time travelling the route of the voyageurs. That summer we paddled through the beautiful Boundary lakes to Fort Frances, at the west end of Rainy Lake, apparently the first canoe party for years to paddle all the way from Lake Superior. We decided, then and there, that next year we would start to retrace the rest of this celebrated fur trade route, but starting from its western end, coming mainly downstream. This pattern now became a theme for our canoe trips in the fifties and sixties, retracing historic Canadian rivers – historic in the sense of having been used in the fur trade or by early explorers.

Historic Rivers with the Voyageurs

The Churchill

So it was that in 1955 we found ourselves flying west to start from Ile-à-la-Crosse, near the source of the Churchill, a point a little south of the Methye Portage, the twelve-mile link between the basins of the Churchill and the Mackenzie. We paddled 500 miles in the next three weeks – down the Churchill, the Sturgeon-weir, and the Saskatchewan to Cumberland House – and flew out from The Pas. In sparing the reader a day-to-day account here of the journey, I should explain that Sigurd Olson has already given a sensitive, book-length description of the whole trip in his best-seller *The Lonely Land*, published in 1961.

Besides Sig, Elliot, and myself, the party consisted of Omond Solandt, Tony Lovink, and Denis Coolican. Omond, one of Canada's top scientists and chairman of the Defence Research Board, was strong and husky – he had played football for the University of Toronto. The other two were also powerfully built. For Tony Lovink, the six-foot-four Netherlands ambassador, the canoe trip was a holiday and a welcome change from his life of protocol. His many eastern postings had included the ambassadorship to China and he had a world view to contribute. Even his extreme sensitivity to blackfly bites did not dampen his ardour for the Canadian wilderness and he has since chosen

Canada for his retirement. Denis, president of the British-American Banknote Company, was the youngest of the party, being only forty. He had a sailor's feel for weather and water and was a great raconteur in English, French, or a hilarious mixture of the two. As the novice of the trip he was assigned the task of chronicler, since his impressions would probably be the most vivid. His account was published in three parts by the Ottawa *Journal*, as were also the descriptions of our main summer trips in subsequent years.

The route is a canoeist's dream, the Churchill section being less a river than a series of attractive lakes, linked by fast water, rapids, or falls. Frog Portage, less than a quarter of a mile, gives easy access to the Sturgeon-weir River, a joy to run with a drop of four feet to the mile and no serious hazards. On our whole journey there were about a hundred rapids, most of which could be shot, and the portages were short and in good condition.

The rich history of the area had a vividness for us, not only because the country was so unspoiled but also because these waterways had played such a dramatic part in the early rivalry among the fur traders. White traders had not penetrated the upper Churchill before 1774, but there was a steady Indian traffic taking furs down to the Hudson's Bay Company. In that year, independent traders from Montreal gained access to the Churchill by coming up the Sturgeon-weir, and in the following two years the Indians coming down the Churchill were intercepted and persuaded to trade their goods to the Montrealers. Frog Portage, the site of this dealing, was for a time afterwards known as Trade Portage, and Louis Primeau, who had been sent by Joseph Frobisher to seek out the Indians on the Churchill in 1774 and winter there, was also requested to build a dwelling for the Frobisher brothers, Joseph and Thomas, at the portage. Peter Pond, Thomas Frobisher, and Alexander Henry, all of whom had travelled together on the Sturgeon-weir, pushed on independently up the Churchill, the latter two to Lac Ile-à-la-Crosse in 1775 and 1776 respectively.

Meanwhile, alarmed at the increasing threat from their competitors, the Hudson's Bay Company, with headquarters at York Factory on Hudson Bay, commissioned Samuel Hearne to set up a post at a suitably strategic point on the Saskatchewan. Cumberland House, which he built in 1774, before long proved to be a key to supremacy in the fur trade.

There are four things that stand out in my memory of those days down the Churchill River: the learning process of how to cope with rapids, our contact with the many Indians we encountered, the reception by the media to the idea of what we were doing, and our relations among ourselves as a canoe party.

The learning process (in the absence of 'schools' for canoeing techniques) proved to be sometimes an exciting one, some of our party having had little experience of white water. We were always being asked, 'But you mean that you don't take guides?' Our first rapid on the Churchill was the Drum, which was diametrically across Patuanak Lake from our first campsite. Because of its distance, it throbbed rather than roared all night. We had written to the various Hudson Bay factors along the way asking them please to consult Indians regularly plying the river as to whether any particular rapids were dangerous to run. The replies indicated that, even at high spring level, all were runnable, with care, and that at all seasons the Churchill was a route regularly used by canoes. What this chiefly demanded of relative greenhorns, we found, was reading the portage *paths* with care. The river at the time we were on it in early summer was running about three feet above its normal summer level. The condition of the portage path became our gospel. We quickly became aware, from the conformation of the land, of where to look for the start of a portage. The path said everything: if the portage showed that it was clearly in common use, we knew that this meant a rapid which the Indians did not run but portaged. This rule of thumb held all the way down our route – a route which, in a land without roads, had been the only thoroughfare for its inhabitants and had been in use, we knew, for ten thousand years, since the melting of the glaciers.

The Drum nevertheless was an exciting run, and I can recall

that occasionally Elliot Rodger and I shamelessly made use of
the high water when we came to a particularly rough-looking
drop, by running the canoe through the flooded willows along
the low banks and perhaps holding on briefly to a branch or two
on the way down, to reduce our speed. The next rapid was the
Leaf. It was shallower, though still fast, and we had been told to
exercise special caution. The rocks were everywhere, and it
seemed impossible, at our stage of expertise, to dodge them all.
Our Peterborough Prospectors took a beating, and when we
took time in an eddy at the foot of the rapid to stop and count
the cost, we found that each of the three canoes had a bashed-
in and broken rib. However, no actual breaks in the canvas were
found, and we hastily went on, for the Deer was just around
the next bend. This rapid we made without casualty, for it was
deeper. We proceeded, with the realization that we had still a
lot to learn.

A few days later, when we had stopped to have lunch at the
top of a long rapid which looked a bit more serious, four canoes
of Indians came into sight on their way down the river, so we
leapt into our own canoes to follow them as closely as practic-
able. Our greatest difficulty was learning to back-paddle and
steer at the same time, but we got the message: a canoe in a
rapid is not meant always to be paddled forward, but often sideways, or sometimes even backward. Basically, in a tricky section
it should go no faster than the current, to allow more time to
steer through obstacles ahead. Keeping behind the Indians,
and imitating them, proved to be an excellent whitewater
'primer', and we had nearly three weeks more and plenty of
other rapids to practise in. Finally we were able to take on
most rapids with confidence, though still with caution. Our rule
of the portage path – and good luck – got us through dry,
without any actual capsizing or foundering. It was great fun.
And perhaps the more so for our being so green.

The second thing I recall is our many encounters with Indians.
It seemed that every Indian owned an outboard motor, which
he attached to his great freight canoe, perhaps twenty feet long.
And whenever we encountered Indians they came over and

joined us. Most seemed to have been at missionary school and spoke understandable English or French. After a casual chat, perhaps no more than about navigation of the river, the drill seemed to be to 'boil the kettle', which did not take long, and soon all of us were sipping tea. We held many an interesting session such as this.

Those Indians less practised in guarding their real thoughts expressed surprise at seeing a group of white men, all paddling, and most of the Indians seemed quite puzzled by the complete reversal in our roles: the Indians with outboard motors, the whites paddling. So used had they become to regarding the canoe as a vehicle of work that its recreational use seemed beyond their grasp. Not only on this Churchill trip but also in subsequent years it became apparent that the absence of an outboard motor was regarded among them as an indication of lower economic status. And a few years later, when we had paddled across the Barrens and arrived at Baker Lake near Hudson Bay, the RCMP inspector, Stu McKim, told us that he had no doubt that the local Inuit would have been willing to take up a collection for us 'poor whites' who had had to paddle all that distance the hard way.

The other matter of surprise to us in the early fifties was the approach taken by the press. When we reached Cumberland House, at the point where the Sturgeon-weir joins the Saskatchewan, we found a telegram addressed to our party from that most enterprising newspaper, the Toronto *Star*. It stated that they had chartered a plane which would be carrying two reporters to interview us at some suggested place on our journey. We had planned to leave our canoes with the HBC factor at Cumberland House and then to have an Indian take our party and our packs in his big motorized freighter canoe to The Pas, ninety miles down river, whence we would fly back home. Our reply to the *Star* therefore suggested they could meet us as we landed at the public dock at The Pas. The interview was continued on the plane while travelling to Winnipeg. We received the write-up by mail awaiting our return to Ottawa: it was a full front-page spread with big headline and photos!

This attention to our mere vacation trip was, we felt, amusing. Had we been, more predictably, a party of young Canadians, what we had done would have been an un-newsworthy yawn. The aspect that had perhaps caught the interest of a hard-boiled press was that the fact that we averaged, as a group, nearly fifty years of age. This, of course, had a different effect on the younger canoeists who began later to follow us: the taunt of youth was simply, 'Well, if those old goats can do this, we sure can!'

Age was probably not the only reason for media interest: for years almost no one had been reported doing anything as adventurous as retracing the early explorers' and fur-trade routes by canoe down Canada's big rivers. There was an element of history, even of romance, that added to the story's newsworthiness. Most of the participants, too, had a high profile. The media's interest, it seemed, could scarcely have been greater had the Archbishop of Canterbury been discovered making a northern canoe trip with the Pope. It was a 'good copy'.

The fourth thing that stands out in my memory was the extraordinary degree of camaraderie we had in this party: too often the stresses of wilderness travel have been known to breed tension or even worse on a long canoe trip. On the contrary, we had all by now a special bond of friendship and everyone in the group had a high sense of humour (even if low at times). But beyond this was the unselfishness. Two loads over a portage was the standard drill: first one man with the canoe, the other carrying two packs, then both went back for the second load. Sometimes if a canoe, for any reason, had got behind, its team might find on going back for the second load that it had already been portaged across by some kind soul.

By now our individual roles and responsibilities on this and other trips had become established. The bourgeois (Sig, if he was with us, otherwise one of us chosen by vote before we set off) had the final say on any matters of dispute, or perhaps I should say non-unanimity, such as where and when to camp, or whether to embark on a long traverse in bad conditions. This arrangement is less dictatorial than it sounds, for the majority

The cooks, Sig Olson and Elliot Rodger, at work

opinion carries weight, but it is valuable – I would almost say vital – to have one person designated to hold this responsibility.

Omond had taken over the catering from me in 1953, but now Sig was apparently happy to handle the task, with Elliot as assistant. On the early trips there had been mutinous mutterings about the weight of the packs under my catering regime, which featured a high proportion of canned meats and canned fruit. Lacking culinary skills, and having no wish to acquire them, I had been only too glad to be demoted to a mere scullion – we made it a rule that the cooks did not do the washing-up. One person from each canoe was on campfire duty, either cooking, washing-up, or seeing to the fireplace and wood supply, while the other looked after tent-jobs.

Omond, whose first doctorate was in medicine, was naturally our medical officer, not that I ever remember anyone needing much in the way of medical attention. He also had the important position of brewmaster. The evening drink before dinner, all chores done, was a hallowed time, and the precious ration called for serious attention. In the first year of our canoeing together, Tony had introduced us to overproof rum, the nearest thing to dehydrated alcohol and obviously the answer for long canoe-trips. It did not take us long to evolve what we considered the best rum cocktail: a daiquiri made by adding lemon powder, sugar, and water, which has now become well-known among Canadian canoeists as 'voyageurs' punch'. It has the delightful property of making one oblivious to the bugs, although there is one theory that the lemon actually drives the bugs away. Omond, however, always seemed to be experimenting with other mixtures, and we suffered rum with fruit drinks, with spices, with beef bouillon, and once disastrously with cocoa. He explained that these aberrations were only because the lemon powder had become almost unprocurable. Our ration of rum was two ounces per person, but we did carry a little extra for celebrations and emergencies. Omond once brilliantly declared a celebration because there was no emergency.

It became a custom with us that each night's hors d'oeuvres should be provided by one member of the party in turn. With weight and pack-space limitations, these tit-bits could only be modest, but they introduced a welcome element of surprise and variety to a necessarily restricted diet.

My own responsibilities included the general planning and logistics, in collaboration with Elliot and Omond. The files would swell through the winter, as we debated various routes, found out who was likely to come, sought information from various contacts, alerted the HBC as to our needs, arranged for advance shipments of supplies, and drew up route schedules. I also did the research, historical and navigational, and made appropriate excerpts from our predecessors' diaries to read around the campfire. On the Churchill trip there were almost too many historic accounts to choose from, for the Churchill and Saskatchewan rivers had acted as main arteries of the fur trade, and as the only means of travel for a wide area. In deference to Tony's horror of biting flies, I did not bring a description of one party's camp at Wood Lake on the Sturgeon-weir, where the bugs were so bad that the travellers spent most of the night standing in the water up to their necks. But unlike us, they did not have tents with fly-screens.

On and off the Hayes

The following year, 1956, there was a general preference for re-tracing some smaller historic river, and we gave some thought to going down the Hayes River in Manitoba. Starting from Norway House, just northwest of Lake Winnipeg, the route that came to be generally used by the Hudson's Bay Company went first down the Nelson for a short distance and then crossed over to the Hayes, which led all the way to York Factory on Hudson Bay. However, some of us disliked the idea of paddling a river which for its last 120 miles flows through an almost flat, salt marsh, and we were discouraged by reports of the low water level on the Hayes in summer and the difficulty of descending its steep Hill River section. What we eventually decided was to work out a slightly different itinerary whereby we would travel some of the nicer part of the Hayes, as well as exploring a

flanking route — a branch of the 'Middle Track' — that had
been in use by the Company before their canoes were replaced
by the bigger York boats after about 1774. To make the distance
for our three-week trip more challenging, and to see more of the
country, we extended the circuit eastward as far as God's Lake,
using a course picked from the map and said to be used occasionally by Indians.

Gods Lake

This year only two of the original Voyageurs, myself and Tony
Lovink, were free to go, so our party of four had two newcomers:
Tyler Thompson, who had just arrived in Canada as the United
States minister, and Frank Delaute, secretary to the Governor
General. Tyler, irrepressibly cheerful and fascinated with the
Canadian Shield country, became a staunch member of our
group; he was my frequent companion on shorter canoe trips,
winter skiing and walking the Gatineau hills. His delightful
wife Ruth, skilled and resourceful in all forms of outdoor travel,
usually accompanied us and opened my eyes to the finer points
of campfire cooking. Frank, a gentle man of quiet humour and
much inner strength, was never able to join us again on a long
canoe trip, for he was shortly posted to Frobisher Bay as adminis-
trator of the District of Franklin.

Tyler nobly undertook to be cook, and proved to be both ambi-
tious and competent; Frank was his assistant. Ruth had planned
the food list and menus, and had provided Tyler with a small
recipe-book, which he carried on a string round his neck and
consulted feverishly in times of crisis. Omond had given Frank a
crash course on the use of the medical kit, which we always
kept to a minimum. Frank was also to be our chronicler, a task
which he performed with his usual thoroughness, honesty, and
humour.

Norway House

Norway House, to which we flew by chartered plane from
Winnipeg, served the Hudson's Bay Company as an entrepôt
for their furs and trade goods, which had to be transported
between the Atlantic coast and the good beaver country of the
west; it became the administrative headquarters of the Company in 1821. The present post was built at the mouth of the
Jack River in 1824.

We set off down the Nelson, which runs roughly parallel to the Hayes and enters Hudson Bay close to York Factory. Its original name was 'Sea River', since it empties into Hudson Bay, regarded as the ocean. Shortly below Sea River Falls, to which we soon came, the river flows with sharper drop through rocky banks. Carrying the full burden of the flow from three large rivers – the Saskatchewan, the Red, and the Winnipeg – the Nelson from this point on was too turbulent even for York boats.

A neat solution is provided here by the Echimamish River, an unusual geographical feature whose name means 'The river that flows both ways'. The reason, we discovered, is that it is blocked by large beaver dams – three when we were there. In the flat swampy terrain, the third beaver dam on the Echimamish impounded a body of water that raised the middle of this river above its eastern and western outflows, the short body of water between two beaver dams being fed by streams coming from south and north. Once the canoes had been dragged over each dam, we found ourselves in still water, as though on a canal, practically all the way to Painted Stone Portage, beyond which point the Echimamish becomes the Hayes River, quite navigable by canoes. The Echimamish was the key to York-boat travel between York Factory and Norway House. Even in the twentieth century, so important was this link between the Nelson and the Hayes that as the beaver dams had deteriorated the HBC had repaired them, using large timbers bound with iron.

At Robinson Falls we found other reminders of the traffic on the river: first two or three old York boats moored to shore at the upper end of the portage, and then a 'railway' consisting of strips of iron nailed on substantial flat-topped logs, which would allow a 'dolly' big enough to support a York boat to be pulled over the mile-long portage.

Logan Lake was where the extra loop of our itinerary left the Hayes, striking east through a chain of small lakes towards God's Lake. Fortunately an Indian whom I had questioned at Norway House had warned us that the portage started steeply, on rock, a mile down the lake, at a most improbable-looking spot. It took us three and a half days to work our way to God's Lake, about seventy miles through attractive lakes with rocky shores. The portages, though, tended to be marshy and showed little sign of recent use; the mosquitoes were legion.

On the second day across we were faced with an unanticipated problem, for Tyler had a much swollen elbow. We all speculated on the cause. A spider? A bite? A boil? Unenlightened, we proceeded on our way, after Frank had somewhat diffidently dispensed some pills, hoping they would at least do no harm. Two days later at the little hospital on God's Lake the swelling was diagnosed as bursitis, and the remedy – rest! Fortunately we were about to interrupt our paddling, at least for a couple of hours, while we did a murderous portage, and this 'breather', plus a night's sleep, may have contributed to the swelling's quick recovery.

God's Lake, though beautiful, was huge and had fishing-camps and many motor-boats; we were happy to see the last of it, for we had rejoiced in the seclusion of our route until now. We were about to undertake what, as I look back, was one of the worst portages I can recall. The Bayly Portage ran (plodded would be a better word) for two miles from God's Lake over to Bayly Lake. It was through a muskeg swamp and without shade. Every step was into water. Once Tyler, looking more than usually wet and muddy, came back after a long absence for his second load and told us he had stepped into a hole, 'so deep,' he said, 'that I had to reach up to put the canoe down.' Considerately he had blocked the portage path with a pile of branches, so that the next man would not suffer the same misfortune. I was the next man. But I blush to say that, unthinkingly, I kicked the sticks away, then dropped into the same hole myself with a canoe on top – a fitting fate.

We sloshed on through. The remarkable thing, as we discussed it afterward, was that though the mosquitoes and blackflies were incredibly bad in the full July sun above us and the swamp below, the 'counter-irritant' of portaging under such conditions was severe enough to obliterate any memory of insects troubling us. Eventually we hit the end of the portage, where

Bayly Portage

the smokers flopped down and lit up. My own reaction at this
point, I am told, was to hand my watch to someone and then
walk, fully clothed, into the cool lake.

From Bayly Lake the Wolf River, not much more than a creek,
led tortuously into Fishing Eagle Lake and then on again to
Precambrian, rockbound Knee Lake. Like Turnor in 1779, and
others since, we noted the magnetic influence of a rock at the
bend of the lake's 'knee', rendering compasses useless.

Now we were back on the Hayes River, but travelling upstream. Above Trout Falls the river became a long, shallow
rapid, where paddling was impossible and we had to tow the
canoes, one man trudging over the slippery rocks of the river
bottom while the other steered from the stern.

At length we reached Oxford Lake and replenished our supplies at the HBC post. It was an effort to leave the factor's cosy
quarters and battle the headwind on Oxford Lake, and soon we
found we were coming closer than we liked to a forest fire,
whose smoke we had been watching ever since Norway House.
The centre of the fire was only a mile or two away – a terrify-
ing sight, for the wind was still strong. We watched spruce trees
'explode' as a tongue of fire reached them. One minute we
could see a tree, and the next it would turn before our eyes into a
flash of sulphurous gas, igniting others. It was sad to see.

We were now about to leave the Hayes again to take the old
'Middle Track' canoe-route up the Carrot River – beautiful
and rocky. This led us to a point we had been waiting for with
some apprehension, the start of a second muskeg portage, the
mile-long Settee Portage, which was part of the winter road
between Oxford House and the HBC post at Cross Lake. Would
it be as bad as the Bayly Portage? Or even worse? We had been
warned that the start of the portage was wrongly marked on the
map and we would otherwise have missed the thin blaze on a
tree; a painted portage sign had fallen down. The portage itself
was not bad, but its soft footing was tiring, and the next section of winter road, which we came to after crossing a small
lake, was not good at all, merging slowly with a small creek in
which we could sometimes paddle but often had to wade. The

water was exceptionally cold, with permafrost not far below the surface.

And so we came to Walker Lake, and thence to Cross Lake, our final destination. We had come full circle, for we were back on the Nelson. As we began to cook dinner, it came on to rain heavily. This was, nevertheless, the time for a drink. All through the three weeks we had been away, whenever this magic hour arrived, Frank had said 'no thanks', and had stuck to tea. Now, while the rest of us were trying to warm up on a hot rum concoction, Frank remained at the fire, cooking. Then abruptly he changed all our misery to loud laughter, saying quietly, '*This* time I'd like to join you guys for drinks.' We were a cheery party who drowned our sorrows before the excellent repast.

Next morning we rose at five to get a start on our thirty miles before the wind rose. We had a hard paddle, against the strong wind, using what shelter we could find behind the islands on our course. As the end of the lake approached, we were treated to a gorgeous sunset on one side and a full moon rising on the other, a spectacular farewell to another beautiful lake. The factor at Cross Lake and his wife were unperturbed by our late-night arrival, and with true northern hospitality insisted on feeding us and putting us up in their house until our fly-out next day.

I had selected this 400-mile loop in Manitoba partly because it offered real wilderness ribbed with Precambrian ridges, was fairly close to Ontario, and was likely to take three weeks to cover. I was, however, aware that we should be treading here and there along some of Canada's oldest avenues of commerce, used by Indian middlemen taking their furs to Hudson Bay, and later by the white traders and others travelling into the interior.

From Norway House to Logan Lake, and from Knee Lake to Oxford Lake, we had been on a regular fur-trade route, used by many famous personalities in the Hudson's Bay Company, such as Cocking in 1774 and later Thompson and Simpson. Franklin came up the Hayes by this way, at the start of his first Arctic expedition in 1819. We were interested by the indications that

the HBC had begun to apply some of the technological improvements which became available from the middle of the nineteenth
century, as evidenced by the crude railway at Robinson Portage
and the reinforcement of the beaver dams on the Echimamish
River.

The part of our course from Knee Lake to Oxford Lake had
given us a feel for the old canoe route, and while the beautiful
lakes and rivers were unspoiled, the influence of modernization
could again be recognized, for the route evidently came into
use again for mechanized winter travel, the caterpillar-tracked
trucks pulling trains of sleighs over the lakes and muskeg, all
frozen hard. Possibly also our side-route from Logan Lake to
God's Lake is now more of a winter route than a summer one,
for the portage landings were in disrepair and any signs of old
campfires were in mid-portage. Certainly we ourselves had
been in solitude.

Between the Churchill and the Mackenzie

Having started down the Churchill River in 1955 from so near
its source made us realize all the more vividly that the
Churchill, long as it was, was only a part of the much longer river
highway that played such a vital part in Canada's first commerce,
the fur trade. The best fur-trapping area was the basin of
the Mackenzie River because of its cold temperature and its
distance from habitation. Tributaries of these vast river sys-
tems – the Clearwater River for the Mackenzie, and the Methye
(or La Loche) River for the Churchill – were fingers reaching
out to a twelve-mile link, the Methye Portage, first crossed by
Peter Pond in 1778.

It became our pattern in the late fifties to retrace variations of
this bridge between the Mackenzie and the Churchill (inter-
spersed with trips down other historic routes, such as the lower
Churchill and the Burntwood, which will not be chronicled in
detail here).

When each year we picked a particular route, we were in-
fluenced, of course, by what appeared from the old journals to be

good canoeing. This was weighed against three practical considerations: we wished to be in Precambrian wilderness; we
wished to go downstream, so as to be able to shoot the rapids;
and finally we had to consider the logistics of where best we
could either ship or pick up our canoes. For our Churchill trip in
1955, we bought from the HBC three Peterborough Prospector
canoes, which the company then moved around the north for us
in winter, so that the canoes would always be ready for our
next year's trip. This arrangement became more flexible after
1963, when I met with the board of the HBC in Winnipeg and
persuaded them to start meeting the growing demand of recreational canoeists all through their western and northern territory
by setting up a 'U-Paddle' service, allowing the canoeist to
pick up a canoe at any post and return it to any other one, at a
weekly rental charge. They responded even more enthusiasti-
cally than I had dared hope, buying twenty-eight canoes the first
year. Almost at once, they were booked up for a year ahead, and
the fleet was expanded. (Unfortunately, because of 'economies'
the company cancelled this service in 1985 and disposed of
its canoes.)

   This may be the place to recognize the great help given us over
the years by the Hudson's Bay Company. From head office to
the most obscure post, they went out of their way to answer our
questions, fill our orders for supplies, arrange local transportation and give us hospitality. The RCMP were also always more
than helpful, and there are many others, too numerous to
name, who also gave us assistance, either on the spot or by giving information or suggesting where it might be obtained.

In 1958 we started once more from Ile-à-la-Crosse, but instead
of proceeding down the Churchill we went up the Aubichon
Arm, heading for the Methye Portage and the route westward
down the Clearwater. This time Elliot Rodger was the only
Voyageur besides myself who could come, and we were ac-
companied by Maj.-Gen. 'Rocky' Rockingham, GOC Quebec
Command, and Art Maybee, vice-president of G.M. Brakely &
Co., Toronto, who had accompanied me on several shorter

canoe trips. Unfortunately we had only ten days to spare instead of the usual three weeks, so had to be content with a 225-mile itinerary. Elliot acted as bourgeois and also as cook.

Through Churchill and Peter Pond lakes we reached the Methye (La Loche) River and, paddling up this fast river, we got to Lac La Loche, source lake of the Churchill. We camped close to the southern landing of the Methye Portage. There was a terrific sense of history, for this had been the route for all the fur-trade traffic between about 1780 and 1820, and for other travel too until about 1885. Reluctantly, the North West Company and the Hudson's Bay Company had had to share this part of the route. We would be following the footsteps of Peter Pond, Alexander Mackenzie, David Thompson, Franklin, and others, many of whom might have camped in this very spot.

With more than a single load each, the whole portage would have taken us at least thirty-six miles' walking, and probably two days; it has to be admitted that to keep our schedule we arranged for an Indian to take our gear over by horse-drawn wagon. However, Rocky and I decided that it would be dishonourable not to carry at least a token load, so this we did, taking turns at portaging one of the 100-lb canoes, seven minutes at a stretch. It did not look as though the wagon would have stood up to the weight of the second canoe anyway. Our two companions scoffed a little, but after lunch they relented and helped us over the last three miles.

The first part of the portage is straight, a flat sandy path through jackpine to Rendezvous Lake, where we stopped for lunch. This small body of water, only a mile in diameter, was the historic spot where the Hudson's Bay Company's Mackenzie and La Loche brigades met and exchanged their loads of trade goods which were going west, to the Athabasca and Mackenzie regions, with the bales of furs destined for the east via Norway House.

Continuing along the portage from Rendezvous Lake to the Clearwater brought us, within a mile, to the spectacular view described by Mackenzie and others. Here the Methye Portage makes a dramatic descent of six hundred feet or more, so that standing at the lip of the drop the traveller looks for thirty or forty miles down the Clearwater valley. One can only sympathize with voyageurs burdened with 180-pound loads labouring *up* this steep hill. We then sped down eighty miles of the fast Clearwater, running its rapids with joy and perhaps too much abandon to its junction with the Athabasca River at Waterways, whence we flew home.

This was the most direct, but perhaps the most laborious way to cross the divide. Reading the early journals of the fur traders we were intrigued to discover that on their way up the Churchill the voyageurs sometimes had to extend their labours even beyond the long carry, since in some years they found that the higher lakes approaching the portage were frozen. Our only echo of this occurrence had been to find, when we camped near the Methye Portage landing, that in the night the considerable amount of dew condensed on our canoes had frozen so that we had to scrape them free of ice – this, during the first week of August.

In 1796, his last year with the Hudson's Bay Company, David Thompson was commissioned to explore a more northerly route to Lake Athabasca which would avoid not only the higher lakes and the long Methye Portage itself, but also a long stretch of the east-west route that was shared in rivalry with the North West Company. Thus, from a point on the Churchill about twenty miles below Frog Portage, Thompson went north up the Reindeer River to Reindeer Lake. After going up the lake for about a hundred miles, he turned west then north, through Swan Lake and the Blondeau River, which he ascended as far as he could, and then portaged westward to Wollaston Lake. Wollaston sits on the very divide, flowing not only into Hudson Bay via the Cochrane and Reindeer rivers, but also via the Fond-du-Lac River into Lake Athabasca in the Mackenzie basin. While this ingenious route had avoided the Methye Portage and the upper lakes of the Churchill, it unfortunately ran into even worse risk of ice on the vast body of Reindeer Lake (the fifteenth largest lake in Canada). For example, when we travelled the course in 1957 we found that the ice on that large body of water (135 miles long and 40 or 50 miles wide in places) did not break up until 18 June – a date too late for the fur canoes. It was probably for this reason that no more was heard of Thompson's shortcut to avoid the Methye Portage.

For this 1957 trip, one of our best, we had a full crew of voyageurs: Sig, Tyler, Elliot, Omond, Denis, and I. Although most of us met quite often in Ottawa, it was good to be together on the trail again, and we quickly settled into our usual routines. Starting from Southend, where the Reindeer River leaves Reindeer Lake, we followed Thompson's route over to Wollaston, and on down the Fond-du-Lac. We were disheartened by our first sight of this river, for there was only a trickle of water, most of the lake's outflow presumably going down the Cochrane. We had to wade and drag for a while, but soon the river had picked up enough to carry us, and provided fine rapid-running through sandstone, with attractive scenery. We took out at Stony Rapids at the east end of Lake Athabasca.

A notable incident of this trip was that of Omond's wallet. He discovered that it was missing shortly after we had left the HBC post on Wollaston Lake. We hunted around for it, on the water and on the shore, and enquired of various people in the settlement, but without success. The young conservation officer was optimistic, saying that if it did turn up it would be sure to be returned with nothing missing. And this is exactly what happened, for it was waiting for Omond at Stony Rapids. An Indian woman found it on the shore, carefully dried the wallet and its contents, and gave it to the factor at the post. From there it had been passed from one air-pilot to another and via Prince Albert had overflown us to our destination. Every banknote and document was there.

Another historic retracing in this general area was to travel at least part way down the Mackenzie itself. Every other American canoeist one talks to or hears from seems to have a compelling – probably romantic – urge to go down the Mackenzie to the sea. Certainly this great river is prominent in Canada's history, starting with Alexander Mackenzie's epic journey to its

Shallow waters at the start of the Fond-du-Lac River

mouth in 1789 and continuing as an avenue of exploration and commerce. We, however, did not wish to paddle its full length. It is too vast, three or four miles across in places, a huge Mississippi of the North, with a heavy barge traffic evidenced by the oil drums lining the banks. Instead of being majestic and rockbound, this river initially carved its course through prairie-like alluvium. Even the water is yellowish, resembling the Saskatchewan's, except for a stretch below the mouth of the Great Bear River, where the central tawny band of Macken-zie water is flanked on one side by a blue stream from the Great Bear, and on the other by a brown stream from the Liard, which enters a little higher upriver. Apart from a one-mile portage below Fort Fitzgerald, the river is navigable all the way from Great Slave Lake to the sea.

We chose instead to paddle a compromise, back route, used by the Indians before the days of outboard motors. This canoe route left the Mackenzie at Great Slave Lake. Passing Fort Rae, it went up Marian Lake and the Marian River and crossed the height of land into Sarah Lake. Thence it passed through a charming maze of rockbound Precambrian lakes linked by the Camsell River and emptying into Conjuror Bay of Great Bear Lake. From here our route involved coasting to the west end of Great Bear and then heading down the Great Bear River. The whole eighty-mile stretch down to the Mackenzie is so fast that it can be done in ten hours. We had no burning wish to travel far on the Mackenzie itself, so paddled it only as far as Norman Wells, sixty miles or so further down, whence we flew out.

This time in 1959 we were eight: the six who had been on the Fond-du-Lac, together with Blair Fraser and a newcomer, Harry Fast, a vice-president of the CNR and a friend of Omond's. Harry was strong and was a more authentic northern traveller than we summer tourists, for he had at one time spent a year in the north prospecting.

Because of time constraints we flew in to Sarah Lake, which gave us a downhill route all the way. But it was far from being a soft journey. We were almost constantly battling a strong north wind, and it was the coldest summer in local memory.

Cold northern scenes on the Camsell River:
left Blair Fraser, chilly, one-legged flannels over his jeans;
right An overcast day in the 'land of little sticks'

Every morning our cooking-pots were iced over. All of us were
chilly, Blair particularly so. He cut a pathetic figure, huddled
in his hooded jacket and wearing two and a half pairs of pants —
pyjamas, jeans, and what was left of his flannels after he had
burned one trouser-leg in a drying-fire.

We also had literally to hack our way through. Once this was
to avoid a roaring headwind on Rae Lake, where we decided it
was better to force a way through by way of a few little lakes and
some axe-work than to sit and freeze, or make a lengthy detour. Then we found the rapids on the upper Camsell unrunnable and the portages completely grown over, so that we had
to line down, or wade in the freezing water, or push and cut
through the tangled willows on the banks. But after about a
week, we came to good portages, and we even had a few spells of
sunshine. We began to feel human again, and to enjoy the
scenery — very northern, with small trees and ice-scoured
shores.

Once we had reached Great Bear Lake, we really were home
free. Concerned about tackling the huge lake towards the end
of a time-constrained trip, on a course which would leave us
exposed to its whole sweep from the north, we had gratefully
accepted the kind offer of the Eldorado Mining and Refining
Company to transport us across to the outlet of the Great
Bear River. They picked us up at Conjuror Bay, took us to Port
Radium a little way north, cossetted us for the weekend and
then took us to our destination on the other side of the lake.

Across the river from us was the site of Fort Franklin, where
Franklin and his party spent the two winters of their 1825–7
expedition. Both in 1825 and 1826, Franklin went from here
down the Great Bear River and to the mouth of the Mackenzie, then back up again; on the second occasion he and Richardson fulfilled their mission of surveying the Arctic coast, one
to the west and the other to the east.

The Great Bear River is a joy to canoe, its speed enhanced by
the clarity of the water, so that the rocks are seen racing past
below. We had fun running the St Charles Rapids down the gorge
through the Franklin Mountains, and made such good time
that we allowed ourselves half a day to climb Mount St Charles,

which gave us a stupendous view in the clear air. We could see all the rest of our course below us, and across the Mackenzie valley to the snow-capped Rockies beyond.

The Mackenzie has a fast and powerful current, fifty miles a day being recognized as an easy rate for canoeists. The very speed of the river, however, presents one of its more unpleasant features. The strongest wind in this latitude comes from due north and blows straight up the river. All who have paddled down a swift river have discovered what happens when a strong contrary wind meets such a current: large waves are formed which add to the difficulty of making headway. Fortunately the real old-timers had met this situation on a number of the faster great rivers of the north, and I had read of their solution in early journals. They overcame the problem by using what I have always referred to as the 'bucket trick,' which consisted of tying strongly to the painter at the bow an empty bucket or cooking-pot which was then thrown overboard. The current, stronger than the wind, quickly filled the bucket and pulled the canoe forward into the wind at a speed that made it unnecessary even to paddle or row. An added benefit was that any piles of detritus or glacial dumps of gravel on the river bed were automatically avoided, as the current swept around these, pulling the canoe with it.

We had chosen the most attractive part of the Mackenzie to travel, where mountain ranges flank it closely on both sides. But in general, we decided, the Mackenzie is not classifiable as 'canoe country'. It is too wide, and the fine scenery of the Mackenzie mountains is too frequently obscured by high banks. But I did return to the Mackenzie some years later. One chapter in its history had been as an avenue for the Yukon gold rush. Most of the Klondikers took other means to reach the gold-sites, by various laborious routes from the Pacific coast. But some instead travelled from Edmonton by road over to Athabasca Landing and thence down the Athabasca, and continued on the Mackenzie as far as its delta. From this point they headed over the Richardson mountains, up the swift Rat River. Wanting to see this fabled route, in 1965 we started from the Mackenzie delta. That is another story, which will be left till later in the book.

Coursing Big Lakes

Paddling the length of a big lake is not everyone's idea of enjoyment and may perhaps be regarded as an acquired taste. And yet it can become a supremely rewarding challenge, a never-to-be-forgotten experience. For me, the initial spur was that some of the great lakes lay on the historic fur trade route. In my trips with my friends, retracing the old waterways, we had creamed off the fun part, travelling rivers and chains of moderate-sized lakes, mostly going downhill to reduce the labour and to have the excitement of the rapids. The early voyageurs, however, had faced up to the great lakes as they came to them, lakes such as Huron, Superior, and Winnipeg. If I wanted to get the feel of travelling the whole route of the voyageurs, I too should tackle them.

Mighty Lake Superior was the one that first drew me. As a matter of fact, I had been thinking of a quite different trip for that summer of 1960, down the Parsnip and the Peace, the rivers travelled in 1793 by Alexander Mackenzie, the first white man to work a way through to the Pacific by canoe. This year my usual canoeing companions were all otherwise committed, and I was going just with my wife, Pam. Somehow, though, I couldn't work up a great deal of enthusiasm for the Peace. Much of the time we would be down in a deep 'ditch', and there were reports that already the surveying and engineering crews were at work there, preparing for the big Bennett dam. Then it struck me — maybe this was the time to do something quite different and take on Superior, paddling the north shore eastward from the Lakehead to the Sault, a matter of 425 miles. The direction of travel was suggested by the prevailing winds, said to be from the west. I had heard of no one attempting to canoe this route in recent decades, although a few people had done sections of the course. The more I thought about it, the more excited I became.

The north shore of Lake Superior was, of course, part of the mainline of the east-west fur trade. We would have three weeks for our journey, whereas the voyageurs, with their *canots de maître*, would take much less time, although, like us, they were at the mercy of *la Vieille*, as they called the wind.

We did not lack warnings against making the trip. As part of the logistic planning, I wrote to post offices at various small settlements along the shore to find what postal and phone services were available, in case we needed them in emergency. Some of these communities had become ghost towns, for the fishing industry had dwindled since the lampreys invaded; from such places there was no reply. At others, the postmistress would answer my requests for information, but lacing her replies with a litany of exhortations not to go. We learned later, from our few chance encounters, that people living beside Lake Superior have an understandable respect for its dangers. An ecologist colleague of Pam's even described how the canoe would become a target for the lampreys, which would attach themselves in myriads to the canoe and hinder progress. A little research satisfied us that this was a gross exaggeration. For myself, I was concerned as to whether Pam would be able to pull hard enough and long enough to let us get through, but we managed it, by averaging 28 miles a day over the fifteen days when we were able to paddle at all. But for eight days we had to sit and wait for the wind to drop.

The big lake tested us right from the start. From our first campsite two miles out of Fort William, even our first four-mile traverse to the Welcome Islands was scary, in the strong

wind on the bow quarter. Once we were out of the shelter of
the channel, the waves were large and the wind was increasing.
Our 17-foot Grumman rode the waves well, but we were shipping water and beginning to realize what we were taking on.
We finally made it to the Welcomes, but it was a tough and
alarming pull, and we were now faced with a long open stretch
to Thunder Cape, quite out of the question in these conditions. So there we stayed all day, poised to leave if the wind
gave us a chance, and there we eventually camped, still
within sight of our starting-point. Six miles in 36 hours certainly
didn't augur well for doing 425 miles in three weeks, and we
felt very vulnerable, out there in a huge bay.

The next day dawned clear and calm, and we were up at three
for what became a frequent feature of the trip: cold breakfast,
prepared the night before for a quick get-away. We learned to be
up and away within an hour. This often proved critical to our
progress, to break the back of a big traverse before the wind
became to strong to handle; and many times we could con-
gratulate ourselves that, had we been half-an-hour later, we
would have been in trouble. (Once, at a frigid, windbound
breakfast-time on the Coppermine, Bill Mathers asked, 'Do you
Morses *ever* skip cooking breakfast?' 'Oh, yes.' 'Boy, it must
be really rugged then.' But it was not a matter of ruggedness –
simply of grabbing good conditions.)

We set off on what we estimated would be a three-hour traverse across the rest of Thunder Bay. The lake was calm, and
the sun rose, fiery red, over the Sleeping Giant. It was an easy
trip until the end of the second hour, when the wind rose from
the southwest and the waves grew fierce. Shipping water, we
just managed to get round Thunder Cape, and into the haven
of Tee Harbour for a brief rest before tackling the rough waters of
the next stretch. By this time there was a strong blow, coming
over a 200-mile reach all the way from Duluth; this early in the
trip we had no idea of what sized waves our canoe could take,
but we were pretty sure that once we got out of the lee of Silver
Islet, just ahead, they would be unmanageable.

As we panted thankfully into the shelter of Silver Islet, we were greeted on the quay by friends who had seen us off, with ceremony and refreshment, at Fort William, only two days earlier. Other friends from the same farewell party soon appeared on the scene. We felt embarrassed at having reappeared so soon, but there was no arguing with the lake that day. One household after another took us under its wing, and we had a restful and well-fed afternoon. And here we sensed already the spell that Lake Superior had cast upon us. Although we had been on our way for less than 48 hours, the complete isolation and the absorption with wind and waves had put us in another world, another existence. Grateful though we were for all the wonderful and spontaneous hospitality of our friends, we quailed a little at social encounters and longed to be out there on the lake again.

Partly for this reason, and partly because we felt we should show some spirit and not overstay our welcome, in the late afternoon we launched again into the surf, though later we agreed that it had been crazy to do so. The wind had dropped a little, but the waves had built up to an alarming size. Worse still, at the narrow exit to the bay, the bounce-back of the waves from a high cliff was formidable, even frightening. Our friends watching from the shore saw us disappear into every trough as we rounded the rocky point. One, a newspaperman, filed a report that reached the national press and was so pessimistic of our chances of survival that we found to our astonishment when we reached Marathon a week later that we had virtually been given up for lost.

Out in the open lake, I remarked to Pam, who has since admitted that she has never been so scared in her life, that I estimated the waves to be six feet high. 'Don't be silly,' she said. Then, a few minutes later, 'You know, I think you're quite right.' Neither of us relished turning back, but what we had to face now was crossing Black Bay, a huge arm more than forty miles long. The traverse would be only about six miles, and once across we should be in the relative shelter of islands, but this was a poor time to seek a landfall on a strange shore, in a high wind and with approaching darkness. To head north into the bay would not help much, for we should be adding many miles and perhaps storing up more trouble for ourselves to fight a way out. Just ahead lay tiny, wind-swept Clark Island, little more than a gull-rock. We decided on a makeshift camp there, gambling that the next morning's conditions might be better. Supper was not needed after our stay in Silver Islet, and we prepared another cold breakfast for a quick get-away next day.

At three, we woke to a rising wind. This rock was no place to stay, and we gobbled our honey sandwiches, loaded the canoe with difficulty in the troubled waters, and set out. The first sheltering island, aptly named Hardscrabble Island, seemed a long way off, and the crosswind made steering awkward. Our canoe was a whitewater model, with a shoe keel which made it very liable to drift. Suddenly my arms were seized with spasms of cramp, and we had to stop paddling. It was oddly restful: when we were not trying to force through the waves the canoe rode them like a gull, but we could not afford to stay like this for long, for we were fast drifting off course. As soon as the cramps had subsided, we bent to the paddles again, more frantically now lest my arms gave out again before we had reached shelter. At last we reached safety, almost delirious with relief, and had a luxurious second breakfast at 11 am. Now for a while we would have the relative shelter of an island screen, and could enjoy our surroundings.

This was our initiation to big lake canoeing on Lake Superior in a 17-foot canoe. Yet these tough conditions gave us a measure of solitude which enhanced the spectacular scenery and added a dimension to our re-enactment of what the early voyageurs faced regularly, as a matter of course. As for danger, we could usually, when the lake became too boisterous or the wind too strong, get to shore and wait it out. Except for a few stretches along the way, take-outs and campsites were easy to find. Perhaps one of the greatest difficulties was in deciding when to embark on any of the big traverses that we had to make. Several of these were ten or twelve miles across – three hours' paddling. We would try to wait until the weather looked propitious, often in the early morning. During the first hour, we had the chance of going back if the wind kicked up, and for the last hour of the journey, the land ahead was within reach. It was during the middle hour, far from either shore, that one felt so vulnerable; and we learned on Lake Superior that a squall could blow up without warning, out of a clear blue sky. In this sense, our situation was different from that of the voyageurs, who in their 36-foot canoes, with several men at the paddle, had enough engine-power to get to shore quickly in time of trouble. In other senses, we more nearly shared their experiences and gained a better understanding of their daily schedule. For example, it no longer seemed astonishing that they usually set off at two or three in the morning, for that was often the most effective and comfortable way to travel on the big lake.

As we, like the voyageurs, paddled for hours watching a land feature shaping up from far ahead, the early history of Canada was brought to us by the names perpetuated from fur trade days. Besides the well-known Pie Island and Sleeping Giant, there were Otter Head, Bottle Point, Pancake Island, Pointe Chapeau, the Paps, and others. One name, though, puzzled us. As we approached Cape Gargantua, we expected to see a towering shoreline, but though not flat, it was not particularly impressive. There was no question that we were in the right place. Perhaps, we thought, the name came from massive hills further inland, for the map was dotted with Gargantua-names, and there was even a Grangousier Hill. Suddenly I broke into laughter, as the reason for the name struck me. There, stretching into the lake, was a perfect profile of a certain human appendage, two miles long. Those voyageurs had a good sense of humour. The allocators of geographical names had solemnly picked up the theme, perhaps not knowing its reason, for the shape of the point's profile cannot be guessed from the blunt coastline on the map.

When we tired of thinking about the shape of the shoreline, we would read pictures into the clouds, or simply let the mind wander for hours at a time. Usually, the clouds that built up during the day would give a perfect outline of the shore, because of the warm air rising from the land. Even each small island would have its 'cloud-map' overhead, and more than once we would locate a low-lying island by its cloud before we could actually see the island. This cloud-pattern phenomenon is often noticeable when flying over any of the Great Lakes in summer.

For navigation on Lake Superior, we had hydrographic charts, which were astonishingly detailed and accurate. Every tiny shoal was faithfully depicted. On the other hand, the inland details were sketchy, and lacked contours. This did not matter when we were hugging the coast, but our schedule and inclination prompted us to make many long traverses. There, even with ordinary topographical maps, it would have been difficult to navigate by mainland features, for one does not have to be far off shore for the points and headlands to merge into the background. Often we estimated our position from our watches, by dead reckoning, assuming an average speed of three and three-quarter miles per hour. If there were islands within sight, they helped to pinpoint our location. This taught us another lesson. Whereas in river travel one can reduce the bulk of the maps by trimming them close to one's course, when travelling on big lakes it is wise not to crop the maps too closely, because distant features may be needed for navigation.

We had begun to wonder, during those first boisterous days, whether the wind would allow us to share the steering as we usually do. Pam and I like to take turns in the stern, swapping places at midday. This gives one a change of responsibilities and of muscle demands, and a bit of relaxation for the bowman, who can afford to look around at the scenery. On a big lake, especially, the stern paddler has at every stroke to concentrate on the objective (which may be only an ill-defined spot on the horizon), and at the same time allow for wind drift. This, plus the physical effort of holding course while paddling, can become quite exhausting, which is why we like to spell each other. But when the wind is strong, or in rapids, I take the stern. We wondered how often, if at all, Lake Superior would let up enough for Pam to take her turn. What worked out in the end was that I took the stern for traverses, and we divided the rest of the stern-paddling between us. Because the lake is so deep, its waves are for the most part broad-based, and we learned to 'ride' the canoe over them as if on horseback. Occasionally it was expedient to miss a stroke or two, or to turn the canoe slightly, to prevent a cresting wave from breaking over the gunwales.

As much as possible, we stayed close to shore, and the vast-ness of the lake was tempered by the engaging little harbours and inlets along the way. Although we failed to see any actual game along the lakeshore, it was apparent that the moose came out of the woods occasionally to bathe and to drink. At more than one inlet along the shore, moose paths entered the beach at both ends, their paths identical, in width and the hard-packed clay underfoot, with portages along the Churchill. One interesting reminder of the fur-trade days was at the University River, where the little bay at the river-mouth was separated from the open lake by a low ridge of granite, barely protruding above the surface. In this ridge was a gap six feet wide, just enough to give easy entrance to a large canoe. Was this, we speculated, the reason why the University River used to be called the Pipe River? Did the voyageurs perhaps seek to take their hourly pipe here, in this comfortable haven along an otherwise unwelcom-ing stretch of shore? The little bay behind the narrow gap would hold a dozen *canots de maître*, a whole 'brigade'.

The solitude and splendour of Lake Superior is most evident perhaps in the stretch of the north shore between the mouths of the Pukaskwa and University rivers, especially near Cape Isacor, where the land rises 600 feet straight out of the lake. One feels dwarfed by the majesty as one creeps along the base of the cliffs, whose top may be shrouded in mist.

We were fortunate, on our first trip on Lake Superior, to be free of the fog which is not uncommon in the summer months. Some years later, on a return visit, we were not so lucky. Dense fog rolled in, and since we had only a few days to reach our objective, we could not afford to wait for it to clear. We could see no more than a canoe-length ahead, and the conden-sation on the canoe, which was chilled by the frigid water, was so great that we were continually mopping up with baling

Near the mouth of the Pukaskwa River, Lake Superior

cloths. Worst is the business of navigating by compass. The compass is set so that the course coincides with the axis of the canoe, and the steersman tries to keep the needle pointing north on the dial. As with walking in a fog, it is surprisingly difficult to keep a straight course.

Our trip on Lake Superior fell into three main sections, with convenient reprovisioning points at Marathon and Michipicoten. Except at these two places, and at Silver Islet, we met no one apart from two Indians fishing, a lighthouse keeper, and a couple of local canoeists as we neared the Sault. The road along the north shore had been completed that year, but was not opened until after we were through. For the middle section of our trip, the big bulge from Marathon to Michipicoten, the road does not follow the shore, being forced by the rugged terrain to go far inland. And even on the rest of the journey, we were not often close to the road, having opted to take an outer course. For example, we stayed outside St Ignace and Simpson Islands, but strong winds drove us eventually to take the Simpson Channel leading to the inner course of Nipigon Bay and the Schreiber Channel. We cut across Agawa Bay and Batchawana Bay, each time to avoid being on an exposed west-facing shore and each time rather with our hearts in our mouths.

Our escape from Michipicoten Bay was particularly dramatic. We had been stormbound there for over a day; thunderstorms rolled over us, accompanied by heavy rain. The next leg of our course, down to Cape Gargantua, lay straight south, and we badly wanted to get past that exposed stretch of coast. Then, towards nightfall, the wind veered and settled in the north, as a cold front moved in. We guessed, rightly, that there would be no better day than tomorrow to make a dash for it. We were on the water by 6 am. Even at that early hour, the wind was strong and the waves sizeable. Our direct course cut across two wide bays, the coast a steep rock wall. Racing before the wind, with hissing whitecaps, we knocked off the two ten-mile reaches and were past the high cliffs before stopping for lunch. The fineness of our timing was borne out in the early afternoon, when a sharp and unheralded squall sent us scurrying to the refuge of a small island. Had we set out much later that morning, the squall would have caught us at the base of the rock-wall, helpless.

After passing Cape Gargantua, the scenery became less spectacular, even downright dull around Batchawana, but it improved near the Sault, where the Shield comes down to the shore again. By pushing hard we had kept on schedule – even a little ahead, for we had to dawdle away a day before hitting the Sault, to avoid turning up before we were expected. A final, unexpected hazard met us at the Sault, when we were holding onto the lock wall, talking to the friends who had come to meet us. A pleasure cruiser roared out of the lock at full speed, throwing up a lethal wash, while a voice through a megaphone blared at the passengers, 'And on your right, ladies and gentlemen, you see this brave little canoe that has come all the way from Fort William.' The occupants of the canoe, casting off in a hurry and striving to ride the waves, felt anything but brave.

Every big lake seems to have its own personality, and as with paddling a river from its beginnings, so with a lake one becomes attuned to it and absorbed by its moods. While Superior is imposing and spell-binding, and yet even kindly at times, Winnipeg is a mean lake, for which it is difficult to find much affection. Two factors make its waves more lethal than most. Firstly, it lies in the latitude of strong winds which blow unbaffled across the open prairies – prairies so bare as to serve as an extension of the lake. Secondly, the lake is extraordinarily shallow: over wide areas the depth is no more than eleven feet, and the average depth, over the whole 9300 square miles, is (I have been told) only forty feet. This makes the waves of Lake Winnipeg sharp, steep-fronted, and close together, so that even waves which are not excessively high will spill into a canoe. Wreckage along the shore gives plenty of evidence, too, of the power of the waves to smash up sturdy motor-boats.

Lake Winnipeg was a hub of fur-trade travel, and the journals give graphic accounts of its malignancy. All the routes followed the shore, as far as possible, for the body of the lake was to be avoided at all costs. A short stretch across the southern end gave passage between the Red and Winnipeg rivers. The Hudson's Bay Company travelled from Norway House, near the northwest tip of the lake, across the northern end and down the west shore to Grand Rapids. There were, besides, two main routes from north to south, crossing at the 'waist' of the lake. The Hudson's Bay Company started down the east coast, then crossed to the west and headed for the Red River; while the North West Company entered at Grand Rapids and stayed on the west shore until they could use the Narrows to cross to the east shore and make for the Winnipeg River.

We were travelling Lake Winnipeg from north to south: Norway House would be our starting-point, and we would enter the big lake via Playgreen Lake, ending up at Pine Falls, about seven miles up the Winnipeg River. The whole trip would be about 325 miles. This was in 1967; Pam and I were accompanied by Bill Mathers, a nuclear physicist who has canoed with us on many rivers, and his lawyer friend Fred Cash. Originally we had intended to follow the west shore, but it looked so miserable from the air that we decided to travel by the east shore, which looked more attractive, at least for some of the way. I think we made the right decision.

Lake Winnipeg gave us plenty of solitude but was short on splendour. Its whole eastern shore for nearly 300 miles constitutes the western flank of the Precambrian Shield, but for much of that distance the rock is separated from the lake by swamps and mud. The first part of our route, as far as Poplar Point, was pleasant enough, with rocky shores and pretty inlets. After this, the shores were scenes of misery where winter storms smiting the low banks had bowled over whole blocks of standing trees. However, the lake did eventually redeem itself farther south, where the rocky points and islands were reminiscent of Muskoka.

Flexibility was called for in travelling Lake Winnipeg. Sometimes it was advisable to paddle quite far from land, to circumvent the great areas of shoal. At others, weaving our way among the rocks nearer shore seemed to be the best course. We concluded that our canoes, drawing only a few inches and therefore able to travel through the shallows, were in some respects safer on Lake Winnipeg than motor-boats. Often we felt as though we were negotiating rapids, and the bowman had to keep a constant lookout ahead for irregularities in the pattern of the waves and the white water that might presage shoals. For a few days, faced with a steady head wind and a flat shore, we took to tracking the canoes, one person trudging along the sandy beach pulling the canoe by a bow-rope, the other riding in the canoe and steering. This was done partly because we would have had to go much further from shore to get enough depth for our paddles, partly to relieve the boredom. A note of interest was provided by the yellowlegs, for there always seemed to be one of these birds running along the sand, accompanying the hauler.

A redeeming feature of Lake Winnipeg is its pelicans. Comical-looking creatures on land, in the air they are pure poetry. Like some other birds, they seem to fly partly for the fun of it and they are consummate performers. With uncanny precision, small groups of three and four will fly in tight formation, wing-tip to wingtip or beak to tail, wheeling, soaring, and diving in a stunning aerial ballet. Dazzling white, they will sit, usually solitary, on rocks off shore watching for fish; then take off and skim along above the surface, beaks opening to scoop up their prey. Another year, at Scoop Rapids on the Sturgeon-weir River a little further north, we saw a mass of white as we came to the end of the portage. There the tiny bay at the foot of the rapids was usually teeming with fish, which the voyageurs were able to scoop out with their hands. Now the pelicans had taken over and were harvesting the fish with ease.

Sun can be an enemy on lakes, particularly big ones, where one feels as if in a vast frying pan. The backs of the hands are particularly vulnerable, and light gloves are a must. So too, of course, are hat and sunglasses. We had to stop for a day on Lake Winnipeg for Bill to recover from the effects of not wearing a hat. On Superior, Pam had been glad enough to be windbound at Pointe aux Mines, for she had a touch of sunstroke even with a hat. And for several baking days towards the end of our Lake Superior trip, we were both quite light-headed from the sun and heat: our salvation was to dunk our hats and shirts in the water every fifteen minutes or so, and put them on cold and dripping.

We experienced one of Lake Winnipeg's savage blows, and it was a snorter. Just a few miles short of Berens River, our half-way point and reprovisioning place, we had to cross a large round bay. Storms were marching along on our flank, edging closer and closer, but we were keen to get to the settlement that day and decided to chance the traverse. Suddenly we realized that the next squall was coming for us, and we headed fast for shore. It was a near thing. The storm hit just as we gained the beach. We dragged our canoes up the sand and literally had to hang on to trees to hold our footing, while we watched our canoes being bowled like toys, over and over along the beach. When the first savage gust had passed, we were able to secure the canoes and take stock of our situation. It turned out to be three days before we could set out again.

Only later did we learn of the amusing little drama going on meanwhile in Pinawa, Bill's home town. Part of Bill's anxiety to reach Berens River was to get news of his wife, who was expecting a baby. The child was born while we were storm-bound. The mother, feeling very fit and excited, put in a call to Berens River, but there they knew nothing of us, for they had not been informed of our change of route. Worse still, the man on the phone assured Bea that if any canoeists were out there on the lake, they could not possibly have survived, for there was a raging storm and one could not see one's hand in front of one's face for the spray and driving rain. Deflated and rather scared, she sank back on the pillow. But in two minutes the phone was ringing: it was a Gimli pilot calling by radio tele-phone. He had been listening to the conversation, and realiz-ing the poignancy of the situation had traced the source of the call so as to let Bea know that he had flown over us and that we were all right. The ultimate example of the bush telegraph!

Such storms apart, the diurnal winds on Lake Winnipeg were even more predictable than on Lake Superior. The cool water, and the big masses of land, heated in the summer sun, together make for great winds by afternoon. We had to reckon to be off the water by two o'clock; by evening it would usually be calm again.

Most people I have canoed with have had an urge to sail their canoe on lakes of any size, partly for the fun of it, and partly to get some respite from the long grind. Indeed, we carried a sail with us ourselves on Lake Superior, together with mast and leeboards. But there, the wind was forever in our face, or too strongly from the beam for us to handle. The one time we had a favourable wind, it died in the fifteen minutes it took us to get our sail rigged. On other occasions, I have found it easy to outstrip, by paddling, my companions who were trying to sail. The one exception was on Lake Winnipeg, where Bill and Fred, with a square sail and a stern wind, got so much lift that they simply planed over the choppy waves, whereas we lost way by pitching into the troughs. Even so, as the wind gained strength they were taxed to the limit, and half an hour's sailing was usually all that could be managed.

There was also the problem of keeping together. On a lake of any size, it is all too easy for a party to get separated, which can have serious consequences, even if each canoe is self-sufficient. In order to maintain contact, the faster canoes have to reduce speed, or the slower canoes have to force their pace, either of which can lower morale and even be dangerous. Some canoeists prefer to hug the shore, while others prefer to travel further out. A single canoe, on the other hand, can make instant decisions about stopping or change of course, without the problem of communicating with other canoes, possibly out of earshot. Whereas the usual recommendation for safety on canoe trips is to have at least two canoes, it is at least arguable that on a big lake it is safer to have only one craft.

Even a smaller lake can demonstrate the need to keep in close contact. Before we had got as far as Lake Winnipeg, the fierce afternoon wind had hit us on Playgreen Lake, only eighteen

miles long and studded with islands. In no time, we were
shipping water, more than we could bale out without going
ashore. We looked over our shoulders to tell the other two that
we were going to land, and to our dismay found that they had
already stopped at an island about half a mile back. They had
presumably tried to tell us, but could not make us hear against
the wind. Now we had no choice – we could not possibly fight
our way back to them in those waves, so we had to make for the
nearest island, within sight of theirs, and wait it out. In those
conditions we should have looked back more often.

As it happened, we had a fascinating afternoon. Nearing the
place where we had to land, we saw that, of all the many
islands in the lake, this one had on it a white tent, such as the
Indians used. Not wanting to disturb a family at rest, we huddled quietly in the willows by the shore, our canoe tethered as
best we could manage in the surf. We could not keep our
presence secret for long, however, for the canoe suddenly broke
away, and we had to drag it back noisily over the rocks. A head
poked out of the tent. 'Come on in. I'm all alone.' This, we
found, was the head of the Norway House band. Elected two
years back, he was trying to get his thoughts in order before
facing the annual band meeting that week. He had come alone
to this island in a rowboat, no outboard – a rare phenomenon –
and planned to stay for a few days. We talked all afternoon.
His English was good: he said he had learned it from the Bible.
He told us of his dreams for his band, of his frustrations in
trying to get the authorities in Winnipeg to listen, and also of the
problems with drunkenness. We asked him about the slightly
tricky passage from Playgreen Lake to Lake Winnipeg, and when
we spread out our map he pointed confidently to the channel,
and told us what to look out for, yet he maintained that he had
never seen any map before in his life. We were getting hungry,
for it was a long time since breakfast, but on this, the first day of
the trip, our packs had not been decentralized: at the make-
shift camp the night before we had postponed the job for a day.
Although we had some cans of lunch food with us, we had
neither cutlery nor can-opener, and everything else needed cook-

ing in pots which we also lacked. Our host did not seem to have anything but a bag of flour and a slab of bacon. Mercifully, towards evening the wind dropped and the sun began to shine through. We helped the Indian break willow branches to make a fire, and he pointed to some good-weather signals in the sky: 'That's in the Bible, too.' We wished him luck at his band meeting, but he shook his head pessimistically as we set off to rejoin our companions and head for Lake Winnipeg.

Lake Huron, which I have paddled many times, is a friendly lake, though to be respected. Its multitude of islands, some with huge areas of smooth clean rock, and most of them well endowed with the wind-trained pines characteristic of Georgian Bay, provide ample opportunity for an unwary party of canoes to get separated in the maze. Huron, too, usually develops a stiff afternoon blow, and woe betide any canoe then caught in shoaly areas such as the Fingerboards. For the most part, though, a screen of islands or an inland channel can be found for shelter when the lake becomes rough.

Perhaps we were just lucky in finding Great Slave Lake to be a benign lake when we travelled it from east to west in 1971; we were defeated only by the forest fires that were raging that year. We had seen the western end of the lake several times on our way to and from Yellowknife or the Mackenzie, relatively low-shored and not particularly exciting. But the eastern end of the lake is dramatic, where steep cliffs march for miles along the southern side. The overwhelming impression is of antiquity. The lake seems to typify the primeval, as it sleeps in the hot northern sun. At night as the temperature dropped, we could hear the rocks cracking and tumbling into the lake. They must have been doing so for centuries, yet the massive cliffs seemed eternal.

Great Slave has many and varied links with the past. The western end carried traffic from the mouth of the Slave River to the start of the Mackenzie, and there was a fur-trade post at the mouth of the Slave, on the site of Fort Resolution, as early

Great Slave Lake in peaceful mood: beginning of smoke-haze
in the distance

Lake Winnipeg shoreline: miles of storm debris

as 1786. Other travel went roughly north-south across the middle of the lake, using the chain of islands as a shelter or guide. In this category come Hearne's return journey from the Coppermine in the winter of 1771–72, and Franklin's first journey to the Arctic and back in 1820–21. By contrast, the more majestic eastern arm of the lake has had fewer travellers. George Back came that way from Fort Resolution in 1833, leading an expedition that was intended to bring aid to John and James Ross, who were thought to be in difficulties on the Arctic Sea. Back arranged for the building of Fort Reliance at the eastern tip of Great Slave, at the foot of the precipitous Lockhart River. He wintered there in 1833 and 1834, and in the intervening year worked his way up the Lockhart, across the Barrens and down what is now the Back River to Chantrey Inlet, then back the same way. Only traces of Fort Reliance now remain, and present-day Fort Reliance is ten miles off, on the tip of a narrow peninsula. There is little record of other travel up the eastern arm of the lake until the 1890s, when hunters, naturalists, and surveyors began to come this way. Rather than using the Lockhart River as an exit from Great Slave, most of them went over the flanking Pike's Portage route, travelled by Warburton Pike in 1889 – a 25-mile chain of attractive lakes and portages, all the way to Artillery Lake.

This was the route we chose. We had started ten days earlier from Campbell Lake, the source of the Hanbury, but after Smart Lake we left the Hanbury and went upstream and over the Hanbury Portage, then down the Lockhart to Artillery Lake. Our companions were Ed Levinson and Rob Shepherd, psychiatrists from Montreal. They were to leave for home when we reached Great Slave, while Pam and I paddled on to Fort Resolution.

There was plenty of opportunity to gaze on the lake from above, as we carried our several loads down over the last, three-mile portage of Pike's route from Artillery Lake. The day before, we had encountered a group of canoeists from an American camp, whom I had advised to take this route, but in the reverse direction to ours. They had started out from the east-

ern tip of Great Slave, so unlike us they had a full load of supplies to carry up the long hill. They might well have been
cursing me for persuading them into such heavy labour. On the
contrary, all they could talk about was how beautiful it had
been on the portage — the sight of that huge rockbound lake
through the small conifers bounding the path.

At the foot of Pike's Portage, Pam and I said goodbye to Ed and
Rob and set out alone on Great Slave. Campsites were easy to
find, and wood was plentiful. Occasionally we were windbound,
but not for long at a time, and mostly the lake was calm, day
after day. We encountered an Indian, hunting moose on shore
from his motor-boat, and asked him if such weather conditions were unusual. He said not, but I have never troubled to
check the statistics.

One day, paddling peacefully, we heard a great noise ahead,
which grew in intensity as we approached a small steep-sided
island. When we got closer, we found this to be the nesting-place
of hundreds of cliff-swallows, which were flying around in
clamorous hordes. Later, at home, re-reading Ernest Thompson
Seton's *The Arctic Prairies*, which describes his journey
through in 1907, I noticed a small line-drawing of this cliffy
island, captioned 'Tha-sess San-dou-ay two miles away (Swal-
low Island).' I had not registered the drawing in earlier readings,
and there is no reference to it in the text. It is as though Seton
had intended to describe the high density of swallows, and the
noise from far off, but had forgotten to do so.

Both Hearne and Franklin (on his return trip in 1821) were
travelling in winter, on the ice. Then, more than now when
air travel is so commonplace, the frozen lakes in winter provided
highways. Even nowadays, the freeze-up signals an opening-
up of the country to travel, and the permanent residents take to
their skidoos or even hitch up their dog-teams and go on a
round of visits to friends and relatives, or just pleasure trips.
'The winter is such a jolly time,' said a nurse who once shared
a charter flight with us; 'everyone goes visiting, and there are
many parties.'

We, however, were far from winter, and were becoming in-

creasingly uncomfortable as we travelled west towards the
forest fires. Everything smelled or tasted of smoke, the sun was
obscured, and eventually ashes were falling all around us. This
really seemed to be no way to spend a holiday, and we decided to
turn back to Snowdrift and hope for a plane. Our friendly
Indian had told us that there were three planes a week to Yellowknife, but of course the fires had wrecked the schedules,
and we were lucky to be able to get out the next day.

I should not have been reluctant to try Great Slave Lake again,
but would not want to revisit Lake Winnipeg. Lake Superior,
on the other hand, is inexhaustible in its appeal. One year we
tried to fit a few short trips on Superior into a longer research-
type itinerary, for we wanted to add some parts we had missed
beyond the Lakehead, and to revisit certain favourite stretches
of the coast. But it proved to be somewhat unsatisfactory, for a
big lake demands plenty of time. Even for a short trip, the
need to allow for adverse conditions robs one of freedom to
paddle as far as one would like. With more time in hand, one
can plan a long-term strategy and take quick advantage of good
conditions to catch up to schedule or even get ahead. This, for
me, is a major attraction of big lake canoeing: it involves a full
commitment to the lake and a constant reassessment of strategy and tactics.

The features of big lake travel – the vastness, the few constraints in finding shelter or campsites, and above all the potential peril from the power of big waves and high winds – are
guarantees of its solitude, so precious to canoeists. In these
days when the rivers are becoming crowded with rafts and canoes, the surest way to be alone with the elements is to travel
great lakes, of which Canada has such riches.

Between Whiles

As I record the memories of my days of canoeing, inevitably
the main trip in each year predominates. In much the same way
as the Chinese attach labels to their years, so also for me there
are labels: the year of the Churchill, the year of the Coppermine ... But this does not fairly represent the whole pattern of
the year or its infinite delights and variety.

From spring to fall, once I had settled in Ottawa, weekends
were for canoeing. Sometimes going only for the day, but
more often camping for one, two, or three nights, I visited and
revisited the rivers and lakes of Ontario and Quebec. During
the first years I was exploring the possibilities, trying routes I
had been told about or working out itineraries from maps.
Gradually a network of routes emerged, to be refined and extended over the years. There was exhilaration in adding a fresh
strand to the network, or in discovering a new and beautiful
campsite; there was a quieter joy in paddling a well-
remembered course and finding a favourite campsite untouched
since the last visit, waiting to welcome me and remind me of
its favours.

Logs were an obstacle in my early days on the Quebec rivers,
until I learned which stretches to avoid or where to get information on blockages. Several times we had to force our way
laboriously through long log-filled reaches or contrive to port-

age where there was no portage path. Once a logging-tug took pity on us and cleared a way through. But one time we decided we were beaten, and made for a nearby farm to seek a truck to take us past the obstacle, which we estimated might be at least two miles long. 'Sure,' said the farmer, 'I'm just driving to Buckingham and can take you. But first I have to get a young bull that I'm taking in. Perhaps you guys could help us.' My companion Hugh Savage, of Montreal, and I were game for anything to get us out of our predicament, and with the farmer and his herdsman we hoisted the protesting animal onto the truck, where he was quickly tethered to the floor by a rope through his nose-ring. The canoe was then shoved in along-side, but at once we saw we had a problem, for the bull was flailing around and our canvas canoe was in danger. 'You'd better jump in and hold him off,' said the farmer. Hugh was too quick for me, and leapt to take the head position, leaving me the rear end. The creature, by now thoroughly upset, vented its displeasure in a natural fashion, and I was right in the line of fire. This went on throughout the bumpy trip, and my shorts and legs were thoroughly plastered. The farmer dropped us outside Buckingham, and as we walked into town to organize transportation back to Ottawa, Hugh took a mean delight in drawing the attention of every passer-by to my disgusting condition, roaring with laughter all the while. We created quite a sensation.

In those years I always had the problem of finding a companion for weekend trips. I had many friends who could be persuaded to come once or twice a year, but few were prepared for more than that; meeting and marrying Pam in 1959 gave me a more dependable canoe-mate. Together, or with various friends, throughout the year we would ring the changes on the rivers and lakes around us. One year we realized that we had not once repeated the same course – there was such a variety to draw from. But this was not due to conscious striving, for there were few waterways that we tired of.

Mid-May, in my book, was the best time to run the Petawawa River, in Algonquin Park. It became quite a tradition with us to do so, sometimes twinning it with a journey up the Barron

River, which runs almost parallel: the occasion became
known as our 'Vernal Rites'. When whitewater novices asked
me for guidance, this was the river I chose to show them, for it
gave practice in reading rapids and a final day of fun-running
with just enough challenge to give spice. One year we even did
the Petawawa on four successive weekends but that, we decided,
was excessive. Sometimes the season tricked us and the bugs
were already bad in May; by contrast, on several occasions we
had to wait for the snow-flurries to subside so that we could
see our way down the rapids. For the most part though, what
remains in memory is sparkling sun and water, running the
long rapids below the gorge, mile after mile.

In the height of the bug season we would usually head for
broad open waters, such as the French River or the Ottawa,
where we could hope for more breeze in camp. We might go as
far up the Ottawa as above Deep River, the Rivière Creuse of
the voyageurs, where they would perhaps have begun to feel the
excitement of their journey to the *pays d'en haut*. Or we
would wander among the islands above the Chats Dam. Best of
all, perhaps, were the many days we spent working up and
down the multiplicity of channels of the Ottawa between La
Passe and Portage du Fort.

Here the river, swift and strong, braids among rocky islands
and tumbles down through dramatic cataracts: it is wild, torn
country. The river is aswirl with boils and cross-currents. Going
upstream, we found, was even more fun than going down, the
exercise intellectual as well as physical, battling to catch an
eddy and so sneak up to the next island, then cross-ferrying to
the next eddy, wondering if we would manage to keep ahead of
the rocks just downstream. We had one favourite campsite
there, on an island which we called *l'Escalier*. There was a long
staircase of a rapid on one side of the island, a more lethal one
on the other side, another in view downstream, and yet another
above the island. The spot first lost its sheen for us when the
mainland on the other side of our staircase rapid was shorn of its
pines, and the land was strewn with the wreckage of a '*coupe
blanche*'; moreover the loggers had thrown a rough bridge across

the river below the island, destroying the rapid there. We felt ourselves a little destroyed. Gradually over the years the landscape recovered, but it could never be the same. And then the final blow – the river was discovered and appropriated by several pleasure-rafting companies. Although we could keep out of their way by using back-channels, we no longer felt alone and we gave up going there.

Through the summer and fall we would paddle the waterways north of the Ottawa, looping from one main watercourse to another. The lakes are surrounded by majestic hills, and the rivers are pleasant and unthreatening. In one of our favourite lakes the green-hued water is so clear that even by moonlight one can see deep down to the rocks below. The loons would always be with us. Several times we saw a mother loon dive with her two tiny chicks clinging to her back. And once, when we paddled silently round a low islet where every year we had found a loon's nest, we surprised the mother sitting. With no time to make the usual plunge into the water beside her, she chose instead to lie low on the nest, stretched out as flat as she could, wings outspread, until we moved off.

Perhaps the days of canoeing in September and October were the most beautiful. Maybe there would be the dreamlike conditions of an Indian summer. Or we might wake to a nip in the air, mist on the water, spangled spiders' webs all around. More than once after supper, as we took the canoe for an evening paddle, the northern lights appeared, gradually and almost unbelievably at first, then magically building, folding and unfolding. And in the tent at night we would hear the Canada geese flying over, wave after wave, the throb of their wings and their in-flight calls never failing to excite me.

Then the winter would be nearly upon us, and it was time to think of ski-trails, and to enjoy evenings by the fire. But canoeing was not far from my thoughts. The correspondence on canoeing grew with the years. More and more queries would come my way, from North America, Europe, Australia, asking about routes, equipment, provisioning, weather conditions.

People would phone or write out of the blue, and it was always fun to discuss plans and exchange ideas. The circle of canoeing friends grew and is still growing – some I have never even met, but we have kept in touch over the years. I have been fortunate that doing what I most enjoy has brought me such good friendships.

Winter was a time, too, to read and think about the historical background. From the time we first started following the canoe routes of the voyageurs, I continued my reading of anything on the fur trade and voyageurs' life – in fact everything I could get my hands on. I had obtained access to the Library of Parliament and at the same time was adding to my own library of out-of-print books on early travel in Canada. There were a dozen or so old-book sellers who specialized in this field, and there was at that time quite a large pool of material for them to glean from, in old book stores and libraries of old homes.

I found that my reading 'fed' my canoeing, and that my canoeing likewise fed my reading. My collection was also put to practical use when we were planning our summer trips: during the winter I would pick out excerpts describing features of the route we would be travelling, and other relevant details. Reading these on the trail or round the campfire gave added depth and perspective. And besides this, the journals raised some intriguing questions, still capable of solution by study of the maps and investigation on foot or by canoe.

From the early fifties we were often on some part of the 'voyageurs' highway', the route used by the North West Company to send trade goods from Montreal to the Athabasca country and bring the furs back. The portages were described in considerable detail by Alexander Mackenzie in his *Journals*, even down to the number of paces on the portages, and were usually in such wild land, so rocky and distant from population centres, that we found them surprisingly little changed.

The question occurred to me: since we had found the more westerly portages so little altered from their description in early journals, what was the current state of the portages nearer home? Old portages should be in evidence, not only near Ot-

tawa, but all the way up the Ottawa River to where the fur
traders turned off it to ascend the Mattawa and across to Lake
Nipissing. And it should be possible to clear up also some ob-
scurities of the route further west, up the Mattawa and over to
the French River, and on down to Georgian Bay, and even further
west, from Ontario into Manitoba.

For example, no trace had been found of the La Vase Portage
crossing the height of land from Trout Lake on the Mattawa
over to the La Vase River which flows into Lake Nipissing. And
though it was known that the fur traders in passing Ottawa
poled and paddled up the shallow part of the Ottawa River, portaging past the drop at the present site of the Chaudière Dam,
there was record also of a 'Second Chaudière Portage' slightly
higher up-river. I wondered exactly where it was.

Early travellers, such as Champlain, had described having to
portage on the limestone near the falls known as the Chaudière,
or 'boiling kettle', along a path so near the water that they
were sometimes splashed by the spray. The Second Chaudière
Portage, a little higher up-river, might be more difficult to find,
for a dam had been built at the falls in the latter part of the
nineteenth century and would have changed the river's flow
above it.

I decided to see what traces I could find on the Quebec side of
the river. The first thing I came upon was a large stone statue
of Father Brébeuf. It was close to the river, and from it a paved
path led across a small park, Brébeuf Park, that had been created at this pleasant spot. Not realizing at first that I was on to
something, I followed the asphalt path eastward across the
small park, to find at its downstream end that, although the
asphalt ended abruptly at the edge of the park, the path continued on for about half a mile. It was rough over the limestone,
but clearly it was an old and well-defined path which kept as
close as feasible to the river bank. At one point, to surmount a
steep rise, a set of crude stone steps had been built and at
another, a low area which would be wet in spring, there was a
small stone causeway. At the lower end of the portage, the

path again came down to water level and could have been the
landing. In these days it is not obvious why anyone should
need to portage here, because there is only fast water, easy to
paddle against upstream. But this is not the level of water
when the voyageurs came by, before 1821. The Chaudière dam
had raised the water level considerably, and of course reduced
its racing speed. This was clearly the Second Chaudière Portage
that I had been seeking.

I found then that Mr Chief Justice Latchford of the Ontario
Supreme Court had discovered the old portage in the early
1920s and had realized its historic and national significance. He
had made representations for its preservation and marking,
but then it had been forgotten. Only the monument to Father
Brébeuf, who had once trodden it, was left to signal its existence. The engraving on the monument, however, made no allu-
sion to the portage itself or to the fur trade.

When the portage was 'rediscovered', the Historic Sites and
Monuments Board of Canada was informed, and in 1955 designated it a national historic site. On the bedrock along the
portage a plaque was installed which, in English and in
French, recounted all the famous explorers who had trodden this
path, as well as the Recollet fathers. The land was given by the
Gatineau Power Company to the National Capital Commission,
which undertook to preserve the path in its original, rough
condition. The fact that it had remained still well-defined, with
its little causeway and set of crude stone steps, was probably
due to its being in a tract of land deliberately kept wild by the
consortium controlling the whole hydro potential of the
Chaudière and its upstream reaches. Probably the only users of
the old path had been youngsters going swimming or fishing.
Within the next few years, the stone steps were vandalized and
shifted, but otherwise the portage lies little changed from its
condition when first used.

The La Vase Portage, further along the voyageurs' route westward, intrigued me, for it had to cross a divide, very marshy
for at least two miles, and such terrain would not, like granite,

Misty breakfast scene on the French River
(Photo George Luste, Toronto)

Canoeing near home: a campsite on a Quebec lake

Petite Faucille (Little Sickle) Rapid on the French River; the canoeists have just crossed the short portage. Here, just below the rapids, long-submerged fur-trade goods were found by divers.

remain for centuries relatively little changed. I obtained the
old survey maps of the area and also had the good fortune to
stumble on an old roadway built on a solid stone footing,
though in soft marshy ground. The stone was clearly not bedrock: the road had obviously been laid down by man. From
this start, I managed to piece together where the old portage
had been. The roadway started at a pond beside the Trans-
Canada highway, a pond connected with Trout Lake. Before this
water link had been bridged by the highway, the pond and its
short connection with Trout Lake were shown on early maps as
Dugas Bay. This old roadway then passed from the south-west
end of the pond in a nearly straight line for about two hundred
yards across marshy land to a small tributary of the La Vase
River. Beaver had dammed the tributary at a point near its junction with the La Vase, making it wide and deep enough to take
craft as big as the old *canots de maître.* For many years trapped
to near-extinction, the beaver were back again and performing
their old function, and this was another key to locating the old
La Vase Portage.

The Ontario Archaeological and Historic Sites Board was able
to confirm these findings from their own early documents,
and in 1961 erected a small monument near the pond, beside the
Trans-Canada highway, with a small plaque setting out the
facts.

Another historical conundrum attracted me one summer to
travel to the area west of Kenora, Ontario, where Lake of the
Woods empties into the Winnipeg River. Here with the aid of
the journals of David Thompson and Dr J.J. Bigsby, I discovered
to my own satisfaction the location of the old fifty-yard portage where the voyageurs crossed a small isthmus to reach the
Winnipeg River. (Thompson and Bigsby were respectively 'as-
tronomer' (surveyor) and secretary to the International Boundary Commission set up by the Treaty of Ghent. Dr Bigsby sub-
sequently wrote *The Shoe and the Canoe,* published in 1850,
a delightfully readable account of their transcontinental travels,
with recommendations for the location of the international

boundary.) Later, I came across an old map which gave confirmation. And this was one occasion when I found also a local inhabitant who remembered his father describing where the old portage had been, and whose memories tallied with my own conclusions.

One of the more exciting (to me) finds I made at about this time was among the many French River outlets, where the channel that the voyageurs used leads out to Georgian Bay from the large western outlet of the French River. The official topographical map showed the 'Voyageurs Channel' as running in roughly the right direction, but as a northward continuation of the 'Fort Channel', hugging the mainland coast. Not only would this route have been unnavigable at certain spots in certain seasons, but it failed to conform to the early journals, which were quite specific about certain features of the route. The correct channel used by the voyageurs was unnamed on the topographical map – in fact it was shown as a 'dead end' blocked by a ridge of rock.

It made no sense to have this channel, marked with rapids and therefore having current, suddenly come to a halt in this way, so I poked around and discovered that the river in fact continued, by a twisting channel and a small rapid conforming exactly to the journal descriptions of la Petite Faucille (the Little Sickle), and also to Paul Kane's 'French River Rapids', painted in 1845. The drop here can be bypassed by a very short portage of only 25 paces (exactly as Mackenzie described it), though at certain water-levels the rapid is fun to run. Another feature identifying this channel as the correct one is a short stretch aptly described in the journals as la Dalle (the Eavestrough). These features had been preserved over the 130 years since they were used by the voyageurs, because they were formed of granite, and the current was not strong.

Later, even more exciting corroboration was provided when a friend, who was an amateur diver and who had come across my account of the true channel, made an extensive underwater find, at the Petite Faucille, of muskets, shot, and other articles of fur-trade hardware. Evidently a fur-trade canoe had been tempted to run the rapid, and had capsized. Later on, I also came across an old map of 1850, on which this correct channel was labelled 'the principal channel used'.

It was not far from here too that I found also what I believe to be the voyageurs' old camping ground, known as the 'Prairie des François', a bit of flat meadowland, rare in that rocky region, that could camp a whole brigade of fur canoes. It is situated at the point in the maze of outlets of the French River where the voyageurs would actually enter upon the big, open water of Georgian Bay.

Such riddles have had to do not only with the fur trade routes, but also with other northern travel. For example, I found it fascinating to attempt to trace Samuel Hearne's route, in the astonishing journey he made in 1772 to the Coppermine from present-day Churchill. Much of his route is easily identifiable and has never been questioned. Some of the track is more dubious. Study of the most recent topographical maps hand-in-hand with Hearne's vivid diary, together with a knowledge of the terrain, emboldened me to add my own interpretations to the debate in the literature. Several of these can be only conjectural, but one example illustrates the impact of actual on-site experience, although it makes no claim to originality.

After the celebrated massacre of Inuit at Bloody Falls by the band of Indians with whom Hearne was travelling, Hearne claimed to have continued his survey on down the river to the ocean, and to have erected a mark to signal his taking possession of the coast on behalf of the Hudson's Bay Company. He described the eight or nine miles down to the sea as being 'all the way so full of shoals and falls that it was not navigable even for a boat', and said that the river 'emptied itself into the sea over a ridge or bar'. This was in mid-July.

Sir John Richardson, in his 'Digression concerning Hearne's route', in George Back's *Narrative of the Arctic land expedition to the north of the Great Fish River ... in the years 1833, 1834, and 1835*, disputed Hearne's claim, from his own per-

sonal knowledge of the river below the falls. To this day, however, some historians support Hearne's assertion. Our own experience on the Coppermine in 1966 put me firmly on Richardson's
side. We were at the river-mouth in the first week of August,
close to the time of Hearne's visit. There is a minor rapid, really
not much more than a riffle, just below Bloody Falls, but after
that the river, so exciting over the rest of its course, becomes flat
and slow, running over soft terrain. It would require a considerable stretch of the imagination to envisage shoals and falls at
any water-level. The picture is more vivid in my memory for
the sight of one canoe of our party containing Angus Scott and
Pierre Trudeau passing us at great speed, its occupants paddling like mad. 'What's the hurry?' I asked. 'We have lots of time
to reach Coppermine on schedule.' 'The river has become
dull,' answered Pierre. 'Now that it has lost its life, I want to
have done with it.' A far cry from Hearne's description!

Other probings and ponderings on early canoe travel in Canada have interested me over the years. Enough has been said,
perhaps, to convey some of the excitement of the detective work
entailed, and the way in which experience of the sort of conditions one seeks when paddling, portaging, or trudging over the
tundra helps to provide the key.

It was against the backdrop of the seasons that the long summer
canoe trips took shape. Usually the route would be evolved
around the campfire during the last week of the previous summer's trip, and generally it would fall into place without difficulty; other times there would be more debate. As an extreme
example, in 1961 when the Voyageurs went from Pukatawagan on the Churchill via the Rat and Burntwood rivers to Thompson, we had not finally decided on our route until three weeks
before we set out, mainly because of reports of low water levels
in the north. But such uncertainty was mercifully rare; the
planning and preparation would go on steadily through the year,
building to the climax.

Each year's journey had its own flavour, its own pleasures and problems. Most vivid in my memory now are the trips in the Barren Lands and the sub-Arctic, partly because they are more recent, but also because their relative remoteness enhanced the challenge. And so it is of these that I shall now tell.

Part Two

THE BARREN LANDS
AND THE
SUB-ARCTIC

*A sampling of journeys on northern rivers
in the days before they were much paddled
for recreation*

The word 'Arctic' in Canada has had a variety of interpretations in
recent years: for example, 'the land north of the Arctic Circle', or
'north of the continental mainland'. Nowadays the term more com-
monly refers to land north of the tree line, a land where the low
temperature and high wind inhibit the growth of plant life taller than
low heath. The tree line in Canada starts from near the mouth of
the Mackenzie, dips to brush the eastern ends of Great Bear and Great
Slave Lakes, and continues eastward to about Churchill, Manitoba.
By this more recent definition, the sub-Arctic lies south of the tree
line, and the Barren Lands are part of the Arctic.

Crossing
the Barren Lands

The Hanbury-Thelon, being our first Barren Lands canoe trip, gave us at the same time our most vivid impressions of this land and our greatest sense of adventure. When the plane deposited us and flew off, we were keenly aware that our only way out was to paddle 530 miles of river which few had travelled, to reach our fly-out point at Baker Lake close to Hudson Bay.

That degree of adventurousness, in 1962, may take a little explaining in these days when recreational Arctic canoe travel is fairly commonplace. Nowadays, a youngster at one of the more enterprising summer camps can reasonably hope for a chance of a trip down the Thelon, the Coppermine, or the Nahanni; newspapers and magazines carry advertisements for commercial canoeing and rafting expeditions down such rivers. Numerous accounts have been circulated or published, and there is little guesswork left to be done, although the trip retains all the excitement and flavour of physical challenge and northern travel. But in 1962 almost no one was doing such things. Perhaps the unusualness of our planned journey can best be conveyed by the conversation between my secretary and the airline booking agent. 'Tickets for four,' she said. 'Ottawa, Toronto, Edmonton, Yellowknife. Then from Baker Lake to Churchill, Winnipeg, and back to Ottawa.' 'And how,' asked Trans-Canada Airways after a pause, 'are they getting from

Yellowknife to Baker Lake?' Secretary (deadpan): 'By canoe.'
There was a stunned silence, then 'You're kidding!'

I had become tempted to canoe in the Arctic Barrens from my
reading and from the fact that it was one of the last-remaining
areas of untouched, primitive wilderness in the world; also from
brief glimpses from the air on our Camsell-Mackenzie trip in
1959, and from poring over the maps. Not that the maps were
very detailed in those days. Eight miles to the inch, un-
contoured, and labelled 'Provisional', with a note requesting
anyone finding any errors to report them on return. The rider, 'If
you return', was left unsaid. The Coppermine had looked most
unwelcoming from the air in 1959 – it was a cold summer and
there were occasional ice-tunnels still bridging the river in July
– but the Hanbury, starting from the height of land near Artillery Lake, and the Thelon, into which it flowed, gave promise of
good canoeing. There should, besides, be interesting wildlife,
for the course led through the Thelon Game Sanctuary, established in 1927 to save the muskox from the fate of the buffalo
on the prairies. We were lent, by his daughter, the notebooks of
W.H.B. Hoare, the first warden of the Thelon Sanctuary. (One
entry in particular, noting that his outboard motor had become
choked with mosquitoes, arrested our attention.)

In the Arctic Institute in Montreal, and also in my own library,
I read all the accounts I could find of canoe and overland
travel in the area of the Hanbury and Thelon – J.W. Tyrrell,
Critchell-Bullock, Hanbury, and others – but only Tyrrell
gave enough detail to be useful to us in navigation. The Tyrrell
brothers, J.B. and J.W., were the last of our Canadian explorers,
and their epic journeys in 1893 and the early 1900s had included
the route we took, down the Hanbury and Thelon to Hudson
Bay.

Another indication of the novelty of our plans was the concern of the RCMP. Superintendent Bill Fraser, then in charge
of the northern division and himself a legendary dog-team traveller, seemed to be worried for our safety. He was adamant
that we should take firearms for protection and insisted on alert-
ing the relevant police detachments along our route.

great
photograph

    With all these portents, we took extra care over our prepara-
tions. Pam, a born worrier, spent sleepless nights reviewing
her food lists after reading Edgar Christian's *Unflinching*, the
poignant story of the slow death by starvation of himself and
his two companions in 1927, on the very river we were to travel.
We decided we should make a preliminary May trip in Algonquin Park, with the other two members of the party, to work out
equipment requirements, detect any weaknesses, and assess
food preferences.

    We consulted Andy Macpherson, an Ottawa friend and wild-
life specialist who would be spending the summer studying
Arctic fox at a wildlife cabin on Aberdeen Lake, on the lower
Thelon. He put us in touch with a colleague, Ernie Kuyt, who
would be doing similar work on wolves, from a base-camp at
Lookout Point, shortly below the junction of the Hanbury
with the Thelon. We were glad to accept Ernie's kind offer to
cache some food for us there, though on a 24-day trip a cache
was more of a luxury than an essential. Seeking to balance the
debt, we asked Ernie if there was anything we could do for
him. 'Just count things,' he said. 'Dens, adults, cubs, anything.
Only don't tell Riddle.' Riddle, we learned, was a predator
control officer, employed by the NWT government to extermi-
nate wolves. We found it amusing that this man, at Warden's
Grove, upstream from Lookout Point, and Ernie, both government officials and the only people for hundreds of miles,
should have instructions so diametrically opposed.

    It had not been easy to recruit our team for this journey. My
earlier companions, after a cold trip on the Camsell and
glimpsing in July the ice-tunnels on the Coppermine, were not
attracted to the Barrens, and I was led to draw from younger
friends. Besides Pam, there would be Arch Jones and his cousin
Mike Reford, both strong six-footers in their thirties. Arch
was professor of woodlot management at Macdonald College,
Ste Anne de Bellevue, a satellite of McGill; Mike was a
geophysicist.

    Then things began to come unstuck. Pam was already out
west, and it was less than a week before our start, when Mike

had to back out. It was terribly short notice to find a replacement, especially one who had the necessary skill, stamina, and compatibility. I began phoning all over the continent, to friends who I thought might be good candidates, but all were already committed. We were getting desperate, when it occurred to me that, if we were prepared to lower our qualifications of skill and stamina, we did have close at hand a very keen candidate, Bill Nicholls, who was comptroller to Lord Amory, the British high commissioner. Bill had only recently come to Canada and was eager for adventure and to see as much as he could of this new land. He had never been in a canoe, but had a sailor's sense of wind and water, and his keenness and compatibility were in his favour. 'But what about his back?' asked Pam when I phoned her. Bill had recently broken his back at rugger and been invalided out of the army. 'He says he's getting it checked out by the doctor,' I assured her.

Finally we were assembled at Yellowknife, and crammed ourselves and our gear into our chartered Otter, the canoes lashed to the pontoons. It was late in the evening, but we were experiencing the northern nonchalance regarding time of day, so close to the land of the midnight sun.

An important question was exactly where we should put in. My original intention had been to go right from the edge of Mackenzie drainage to Hudson Bay, completely crossing the Barren Lands. We would fly to the east end of Clinton-Colden Lake, carry over the short (400 yards) Hanbury Portage, then paddle down the Hanbury and Thelon to Baker Lake on Chesterfield Inlet of Hudson Bay. At that time, there was one scheduled flight a week from Baker Lake to Churchill, so the only charter involved would be the 250-mile flight from Yellowknife at the start. But the spring breakup was late that year and there were reports of ice on Clinton-Colden Lake; and now that Bill had joined the party, we had no choice. We must do nothing unnecessary, but get off to a clean start, not knowing what rate of travel we could hope to keep up. So we elected to start at Sifton Lake, a little to the east of Hanbury Portage.

It was close to midnight when we reached Sifton, though it

was still fairly light. The water looked alarmingly shallow for a plane-landing, but after three passes the pilot was satisfied and put us down on a low shore opposite Muskox Hill, so named by Tyrrell in 1902 for the herd that his party had found and slaughtered there. A quick unloading, and the plane was off, the pilot evidently anxious to escape from the clouds of mosquitoes that now assailed us. They seemed, however, to be more interested in getting shelter from the wind than in biting us.

Almost at once we learned one of the lessons of the tundra: don't put anything on the ground without a marker. I had dropped my brown leather sunglasses-case. Although it could only have fallen within an area of two or three square yards, it took all four of us some time to spot it, camouflaged by the grey-brown mosses and dwarf shrubs. The Mounties had warned us to put daubs of yellow paint on our khaki headnets and to take spares; now we could see why. This, too, is why a tablecloth is essential, with a firm rule to put no food or cutlery down unless on the cloth or on a canoe.

markers in tundra

Our two tents were soon up, and we decided to 'sleep in' next morning till 7 am, to make up for the late night. But by 3 o'clock most of us were wakened by the heat and the blazing sun on the tents. And yet, it sounded as though it was raining! Gradually it dawned on us that the 'raindrops' were merely mosquitoes battering at the tent from outside.

We woke to a calm lake and were glad to get out on it and on our way. So flat in appearance from the air, the country around us now revealed its rolling hills, visible for miles in the clear air. It was not until later that day that we began to be surrounded with more vivid colour, and this persisted for the rest of our journey – in fact, we have never experienced such a profusion of flowers on any northern canoe trip since. There were the creamy-white of dryas, the gold of potentilla and Arctic poppy, and the blues, mauves, and purples of all manner of dwarf species – lupins, campions, rhododendrons, pinks. Harebells nodded in the breeze, and dazzling white patches of bog-cotton warned us of marshy ground. Bees worked incessantly over the flowers, often great cushions of tiny blooms which occurred in clumps rather than a continuous spread. The coloured carpet was supplied by the ledum and brilliant yellow lichens.

The sky was blue, the lake was dazzling, there was just enough breeze on the water to keep the bugs at bay, and we felt good. There was a little current, increasing where the course narrowed. We began to sense the glory of the Barren Grounds, the feeling of openness to the sky and of being on top of the world. Sandy eskers showed up miles away like cliffs of gold.

Bill tried to fish at lunchtime, but snagged his line too often in the shallows. We had to discourage trolling, too – we were going too slowly to allow time for that. In fact, we laid down some ground rules: no fishing unless the fishermen were ahead or the party was windbound. I consider it important on a canoe trip to have a schedule, which should be both realistic and comfortable, allowing for fast travel on swift runnable water, slower going where rapids have to be inspected or portaged, and possible delay by wind on large lakes, with a few days in hand for emergencies or side trips. Such a schedule, carefully followed, is essential on any wilderness trip with a limited time-frame or a final rendezvous to make with a plane. One can then tell at an early stage whether more effort is required to reach the objective or whether one can afford to dawdle. Indeed, we had an example before us of what happens without a proper schedule, for at Baker Lake we would be seeing the grave of Arthur Moffatt who, leading a group of young Americans, let the days slip away too easily on the Dubawnt River in 1955, later forcing the party into risks that proved fatal. Our maximum distance in a day was 25 miles on the Hanbury; on the Thelon it was much more.

pace

The early voyageurs would stop every hour for a five-minute break, which came to be known as a *pipe*, and we do the same but without smoking. Pam and I preferred to take a floating *pipe*, to save time and to avoid bugs, but the other two liked to land and stretch their cramped legs, and Bill found it helped his back to lie down. It was on one of these occasions, the first afternoon, that Arch suddenly shouted 'Wood!' and we hurried ashore to help gather up this precious find, old, dense and dry. We shall never know whether it had grown there or whether it was driftwood or left by man. From the air we had seen no trees in this general latitude, and the early journals spoke of none. We saw no more at any place along the shore until we reached the foot of Lac du Bois, where the trees officially, though sketchily, started. Our trove, used judiciously, served us for two days, a real piece of luck. We had a couple of small primus stoves, but had allowed ourselves only a gallon of fuel for the entire journey, reckoning on wood from Lac du Bois down to Beverly Lake.

The river was turning and twisting through broadenings and small lakes, and we had our first experience of the problems of navigating in the high north, where one tells direction by the sun rather than by a compass (which persists in pointing to the magnetic pole, instead of due north). Arch, the forester, would do complicated sums to allow for the considerable declination, but the answers did not always agree with what the sun said. After paddling down a long bay to its blind end we eventually sorted out where we were and got back on course.

On the second day we came to our first real rapid. It was boisterous enough at the start to require lining, but halfway down we were able to get back into our canoes and run the last stretch. Our success, however, and the fun of running, made Pam and me overconfident on the next rapid, leading into Lac du Bois. The first part we portaged; the lower part was a real rock garden that we were wrong to enter, but we thought the high water would cushion us over. Unfortunately Pam, in the bow, was at that stage relatively inexperienced in white water, and allowed her eyes to stray too far ahead instead of concentrating on more immediate obstacles. One big rock just below the surface caught us at a difficult twist in the flow. We went up on it and then tipped sideways into a proper capsize. This was our first Arctic wetting, about which we had read frightening tales, such as that two minutes was the limit of human endurance in Arctic waters, but we were soon relieved to find that this was just another exaggeration. We were hip-deep in the rapid for

Arch Jones, wearing a headnet, with a precious find of wood

about twenty minutes retrieving the canoe and gear, and did
not experience anything very dire. In retrospect, we came to
realize that the combination of shallow rapids and twenty
hours' sunlight a day warmed the water to a sustainable temperature. When we looked at our companions, who had been
portaging, we saw that they were convulsed with laughter, evidently thinking that we had no problem great enough to neces-
sitate their wading into the rapid to our rescue. Arch, in any
case, was busy filming, getting movie footage which he later
dangled before us, at a price. Bill had a field day reeling in fish
after fish, while we spread out the gear and food to dry, no
problem in the dry Arctic air. Everything had been lashed in, and
we had lost nothing but two spare headnets.

At Lac bu Bois we competed to be the first to see real trees.
They proved to be at 'Grove' Rapids, and were an aged, stun-
ted clump that we felt it would be a crime to plunder. The portage into Hanbury Lake was long, tortuous, and hot, and at its
end we were astonished to find the sturdy wooden marker set up
by Radford and Street, evidently only a few months before they
were murdered by their Eskimo assistants in 1912. The chips
from shaping the post were still lying around its base, chips
and shavings that had lain there for fifty years in this land where
the cold, dry air inhibited rot.

This was the first seriously demanding portage for Bill, and he
was obviously finding it tough. Pam asked him if he really felt
all right, and how much the doctor had said he could undertake.
'Well, actually,' he said, a bit sheepishly, 'I never asked him. I
just phoned up and said I was going with you.' He vowed he
would be all right, provided he could have his little rests. To
compensate for his fused vertebrae, he must have developed
enormously strong leg muscles, for instead of just swinging the
second pack on top of the first, at a portage, he would pile the
two packs up on the ground, sit down, slip his arms into the
straps of the lower pack and his head into the tumpline, and get
up with the 120-pound load from a sitting position. It had
been hot all the way so far, and by now must be in the nineties.
Butter spurted out like beer when the can was opened, its

surface immediately thick with blackflies. Arch and Pam ate the
flies in the butter without caring, regarding them as protein;
Bill and I, more squeamish, decided the other two were bushed.
We swam at the end of this portage, but the onslaught of
blackflies on bare flesh made it a doubtful pleasure.

For a day or so after our capsize we were all perhaps overcau-
tious with the rapids, but we soon had some glorious running.
One particularly good rapid above Hoare Lake was a real whitewater challenge. Around here, we began to be hit by squalls
or rain-showers, but they were always brief. Each one, too, declared itself from far away, as a gentle veil sweeping the sky
below the oncoming cloud. We dried out so quickly afterwards
that often we did not even bother to put on raingear.

The walking was surprisingly good at the portages, often on
caribou trails. We had wondered how we would find our course
at portages, but with air photos, maps, and the clear visibility
it was an easy matter. We had learned not to put anything
down along the portage without marking the spot with a paddle,
its blade stuck upward: even a large pack placed on what appeared to be a ridge would otherwise melt into the tundra
background.

By now our daily routine was streamlined to near-efficiency,
and we were in good trim. Up at 5 am, we breakfasted well,
and could be off by 7 o'clock. Sustained by glucose tablets at our
pipes and portages, we would lunch at about noon, making
just an hour's stop. At 'teatime' the snack was supplemented by
chocolate, dried fruit, or cheese. There was a delightful freedom from the accustomed pressure of having to make camp
before dark, though commonsense directed an early enough
camp to get a good eight-hour sleep. Over drinks, I would sometimes read out any relevant passages of the Tyrrells' journal.

Campsites were glorious on the Hanbury, with flat ground and
low heath, and once even a small group of tiny trees from
which we took only sparingly, conscious of the time it had taken
them to grow. Firewood is, of course, a problem in the Barren
Lands. We made a practice of carrying a special sack to hold any
finds we made en route. Hundreds of years ago, evidently, the

struggling forest had advanced a short distance beyond its present northern limit. We became alert for sufficient quantities
of wood to warrant stopping. Further down, the Thelon is bordered for a while with quite sizeable trees, and in Beverly Lake,
the first big lake after the Thelon's long stretch of running free,
the shores are strewn with driftwood, as is also the shore at
the western end of the next lake, Aberdeen. Failing this, willow
and buckbrush (dwarf birch) usually have enough dead twigs
and small branches to provide adequate fuel.

Now the serious, sometimes unrunnable rapids, coming down
from Sifton, were replaced by long stretches of good running.
Here the Hanbury flows through an area of glacial overburden,
where ten thousand years of flow have worn down any steep
drops. The river bed, instead of granite, is softer soil. We had
only to keep studying the banks, and where the soil was clearly erodable we found it was safe to run the rapids, sometimes for
a mile or more at a stretch, playing the river bends wide, con-
fident that there would be no dangerous drops and that the ear
would in any case give warning of where it was necessary
either to stand up in the canoe or to land and inspect ahead.

Arctic terns danced and wheeled overhead, with dashing jaegers in ones and twos. Plovers ran along the banks, and Arch
caught a bewildered plover chick in his hands. We were per-
turbed about the Canada geese, which we seemed always to be
herding downriver ahead of us in increasing numbers. Unlike
the ducks, which could wing back to their young behind us,
the geese were moulting at that time and could not fly.

Soon we were at Macdonald Falls, where the Hanbury starts
its plunge down the 550-foot escarpment to join the Thelon.
Here we camped, for we were anxious to rise early and feel fresh
to take on our one long, three-mile portage past Dickson Canyon, which starts at a bend in the river just below Macdonald
Falls. This is a dangerous spot, and every year has its sorry
harvest of drowned caribou which in swimming the river fail to
notice its sharp turn and sudden drop into the great waves of
the boiling canyon. Neither the Tyrrells' journal nor any other
account had given any advice on the route for this formidable

Looking down to the Hanbury River, at the start of
the Dickson Canyon

nice photos

Arctic evening light on the island below Dickson Canyon

carry, but caribou paths and close contact with the lip of the
canyon made the portage fairly obvious. From its highest
point, the path veers away from the canyon, but one can see
clearly, a mile away, the foot of the portage beside a cut esker.
We lunched midway, all of us parched in the heat. Since we had
not thought to carry drinking-water from the river, we settled
for brown bog-water. The only mishap was that Pam sprained
her ankle, badly enough that she could no longer portage that
day. With the expertise of a footballer, and with almost our entire supply of elastic bandage, Arch taped it up. The accident
proved to be the turning-point in the rehabilitation of Bill's
back. Faced with the emergency, he pitched in stoically, making, if anything, more carries than anyone else, apparently without damage to himself.

At the end of the Dickson Portage, and opposite the esker cut
by the river, was a small rocky island, its surface bare of shelter. This was near where the river debouched from the canyon
into calmer waters, and we had read tales of the prevalence of
wolves and Barren Ground grizzly in the area, looking for a free
meal of drowned caribou. We felt it might be prudent to camp
on the little island, which just gave space for two tents. We
knew that the wolves would keep clear of us, but feared that
grizzly might come after our food.

Above the escarpment we had just descended lay a canopy of
cloud, its dark purple contrasting dramatically with the
golden-green light of an Arctic sunset, a quality of light that
comes rarely but unforgettably in the north.

We were now approaching the junction where the Hanbury
flows into the Thelon, and the start of the Thelon Game Sanctuary. We began to encounter muskoxen and wished to stalk
them for photographs, but here we found we were thwarted by
an amusing situation. Bill had just come from Malaya, and he
could not rid his mind of their resemblance to water buffalo,
which are dangerous beasts. Any attempts by the rest of us to
get close to muskoxen were foiled by Bill's cries of alarm.

We had enjoyed truly splendid scenery all the way down the
Hanbury, with its stark eskers and its rapids but, as the river

approaches the junction, it becomes even more dramatic. First it
flows into a gorge, at the end of which it drops sixty feet over
Helen Falls. We were apprehensive entering the gorge, since the
water increased in speed, and we did not want to get trapped
into dropping over a cataract. On a subsequent trip down the
Hanbury, we were able to run and line much of this section
along the left bank, coming out on a splendid open campsite on
flat rock just above the falls. This time, however, we were hit
by a thunderstorm and decided to portage right past the falls and
the rapids below them. Up on top, opposite the falls, we found
that some government wildlife officials had built a cairn some
years before with a note in a tin box telling who they were and
when they had passed. We added our own record. On our second
visit eleven years later we found that there were more than a
dozen additional notes. Several who followed us wrote that it
was we who had built the cairn, but we had found it there
already in 1962. I should add that on our second trip we discovered that the cairn had been demolished, and the notes were
scattered. From the size of some of the stones that were moved,
only a grizzly bear could have been responsible. We rebuilt the
cairn and restored the messages to their tin box.

Arch preferred, on long portages, to go right over in one carry,
rather than making a *posé* partway across. On this occasion,
he came back from the foot of the portage with the news that we
had company. We experienced a quick wave of dismay, for we
already felt we had become one with this land and resented
intruders. It was no intruder, though, but Ernie Kuyt, who
had made a special trip up in a motor-boat to fish until we arrived, in case we needed help. We invited him to dinner with us
where we had planned to camp just below the junction with the
Thelon, and he reciprocated generously when we reached
Lookout Point a few days later.

Below the junction we were conscious of the much greater
flow of the Thelon. The terrain, too, had changed, for the
banks rose some distance back from the water's edge, and the
beaches were sandy. We missed the high uplands of the Hanbury, and the clean rock or heath at campsites. Goose-droppings

were everywhere. There were compensations, though, particularly in the many sightings of small herds of muskoxen, twenty
or thirty animals at a time. We would come upon them bask-
ing below the bluffs, sometimes rolling in the sand, sometimes
just chewing the cud. When we got too close, they would
scramble up the sandy banks with surprising speed and agility.
One sizeable herd went into its characteristic defence formation, the bulls, heading outwards, forming a ring around the
cows and calves. This is a satisfactory defence against wolves,
but makes the muskox particularly vulnerable to rifle fire. It was
the ruthless destruction of muskoxen after the First World
War that caused the government to step in and protect them by
establishing the sanctuary.

The trees became quite tall and more dense. We slipped quietly past Riddle's cabin at Warden's Grove, not wishing to be
quizzed about any wolves we might have seen, for our allegiance
was with Ernie. The cabin was well tucked away, and there
was no sign of occupation. (Strange to think, as we later looked
back, what a hive of activity this spot was in 1978, when part
of the Russian satellite *Cosmos* landed nearby.) We did in fact
see quite a few wolves on the Thelon. Once, some distance
ahead, we saw four white wolves in pursuit of a caribou. When
we reached the spot, there was the caribou on the bank, unable
to rise, for the wolves had begun their feast while the caribou
was still alive, and his back and haunches were a mass of
bloody, quivering flesh. Here we found our first and only use for
Bill's revolver, a purpose that we had not brought it for. We put
the caribou mercifully out of its misery. We could do no more
for it.

Not far from the wildlife cabin at Lookout Point we came on a
wolf den which was dug in the sand of the high river bank.
The pups were playing outside the entrance, but retreated into
the den on our approach. At this point the mother wolf emerged,
ran down to the river, and swam across. She continued to
call to the pups from time to time, but always kept to the
opposite shore. We camped a little further down that night, on a
broad beach bordered by trees. Something caused us all to be

awake around 2 am, and we became aware that we had visitors. Three wolves, two of them quite young, were exploring our campsite, moving silently like grey ghosts in the dim light. Fortunately we were down wind from them. All of us lay with our heads to the tent door-netting, watching. There was a moment of alarm when one of the young ones made for the food packs stored under the canoe, but they had been tightly strapped up, and a loose rope made a more interesting plaything. Then the wolves turned to the cooking-pots near the fireplace, filled with water as a precaution against a blow-away. One wolf took a billy-can in its mouth, shook the water out of it, and ran off with this new toy. It took us some time to find it again next day. Then they left, silently, but during the night we heard their calls.

Shortly below Warden's Grove is Hornby Point, and the cabin nearby where John Hornby and his two young companions, Christian and Adlard, lost a lingering battle against starvation in 1927, after a poorly organized attempt to winter there. We stopped to look for what traces remained of their ordeal. It was a cool day, we were tired after a long paddle, and we badly needed our afternoon snack, but it seemed a little unfeeling to be munching chocolate there where dry bones and old scraps of leather had been their only sustenance in their last weeks of life.

The trees became shorter and less dense as we headed on towards the big bend at Lookout Point; we were not sorry to see them dwindle, for we had come to love the 'land of little sticks', and the tall conifers had seemed somehow confining and depressing. We made good progress in the fast water. Ernie was waiting for us at Lookout Point, and gave us a splendid meal: fresh cabbage was by this time a welcome luxury. We retrieved our seventy pounds of supplies from his cache, a high platform behind the cabin. Ernie proudly showed off the two gyrfalcons he had reared and tamed. A reserved man, it was not until after the meal and drinks that he sought to satisfy his curiosity. 'I hope you don't mind my asking, but how much is it costing you to come in here?' 'For food and transport, and hotels en route, I'd say about $1200 each,' I replied. With a happy smile,

he murmured, 'And to think they *pay* me to be here!' This was
his chosen way of life, and this was his empire.

A short distance below Lookout Point we came on an interesting variant in the river's flow: it braids here through a stretch
of small islands which are flat and only a little above water level.
In the early part of summer they are verdant with a short
grass. These are named the Ursus Islands, from the fact that at
this particular time of year they are the resort of Barren
Grounds grizzly, and for a very special reason. Their flat grassy
surface attracts flocks of Canada geese, because it offers both
good nesting and also the grass which is their main item of food.
The geese at this season, when they are nesting, have only just
completed their migration from the south, many of them for
thousands of miles, and their pinions are frazzled and tattered.
Nature at this time gives them a moulting period that exactly
coincides with the rearing of their young. This means that
while the grass is green and luscious, the geese cannot fly, and
until new pinions grow they can only run along the level
ground. They become vulnerable to grizzlies, which can easily
outrun them, and prey also on the nestlings. It is therefore a
favourite feasting time for the bears.

An American friend once counted, he said, over a hundred
bears in one day here. We saw far fewer, and it seems that the
peak may last only a few days. Our closest contact was in 1973,
when we spotted a Barren Grounds grizzly swimming across a
small bay, apparently unaware of us and heading for some geese
by the shore. We turned our canoes and paddled quietly to
make for almost the same spot. The bear landed, then became
aware of us, and climbed down the bank towards our canoes,
which were nosed into shore. He could not scent us, for we were
downwind, but his curiosity and poor eyesight impelled him
to touch us if he could reach. A great paw, armed with a battery
of claws, came out towards the bowmen. We figured at this
point that his next step might be into a canoe, and we began to
back off, but here he perhaps caught his first whiff of our
scent, and turned and fled.

Many people now canoe down the Hanbury-Thelon route –

for its beauty, its herds of wild animals, and because it is an easy introduction to Barren Lands travel. Perhaps more would make this trip except that, for 150 miles near the end, the travel is through three large lakes, where one is particularly vulnerable to strong polar gales. Our own experience was bad, for as we entered Beverly Lake, the first of the three, we were hit by strong northerly winds, crossing our route. We did our best to hug the north shore of the lakes, but with their low shores and total absence of trees they afforded little protection. The Thelon, as it left Beverly Lake, headed straight north, into the gale. It promised very slow going – if we stayed on the river. Fortunately close examination of the map offered an alternative – at least for a short distance – for a long bay on Beverly's north shore reached north and almost met another bay further along the river, with only a short and unobstructed carry over the quarter-mile of tundra between them. It put us back on the river, at a bend in the narrows between Beverly and Aberdeen, where the current was strong and in our favour, and where our course turned away from due north and became more easterly.

At the narrows entering Aberdeen Lake we made for Andrew Macpherson's cabin, where he had been spending the summer with an Inuit assistant and his young son, perhaps ten years old. We sat on the low bank and had lunch together. During lunch a rather extraordinary incident occurred. Two long-tailed jaegers appeared, in pursuit of a Lapland longspur, about the size of a small sparrow. The little bird tried desperately to gain height in the strong wind, to get above its pursuers, so that they could not swoop down on it. Then the jaegers began to act as a team and dived in turn, the longspur always just evading their talons. All at once the small bird gave up. We were sitting on the top of the bank, our legs dangling down. The longspur suddenly dropped like a stone under our knees and crouched there, while the thwarted jaegers turned away. It was a rare instance of trust replacing fear of man.

After lunch we had to resume our alleged progress. A peninsula now stretched eastward, forcing us out into the gale-swept main body of Aberdeen Lake. This would blow us away from the relative protection of the north shore, whereas a portage across the base of the peninsula would put us back under the shore's slight protection. Andy and his assistant each picked up a load, to help us. Entirely logically, the Inuit first threaded our paddles crosswise through the straps of the lower pack, leaving his hands free. We gazed in astonishment – why had we never thought of doing that? The answer was, of course, that we have usually to portage among trees. Ever since, when the opportunity has arisen, we have done the same, calling it an 'Eskimo portage'.

Crossed paddles on pack

The weather had become miserable. On our sweltering days on the Hanbury, we had longed for cooler weather or for ice to put in our evening drinks; now we had ice-banks all along the shore, but were too cold to appreciate them. Perhaps in sunny weather Aberdeen Lake can look attractive, but under chilly cloud and high wind it was bleak in the extreme. We camped early at what we called Glacier Campsite, hoping for better weather next day and an early start. To cheer and perhaps warm ourselves, we started a round of Scottish dancing, and picked our way through a Petronella among the ice-patches. Pam made what she admitted next day was a mistake by suggesting that, to speed up our get-away in the morning, we should go to bed partly dressed. The result was one of our coldest nights ever. However cold one may feel at bedtime, the fact is that one's clothes retain a certain amount of moisture, and sleeping in them is not a good idea. The real northern experts advocate sleeping in the buff, and although this takes considerable willpower on a chilly night, it certainly works.

Next day brought no change in the weather, and we inched on. But now we had a fresh problem, for Bill was not well. Whether it was a bug, or delayed exhaustion from his effort on the Dickson portage, or a chill from the night before, I do not know. In my experience, something like this often happens to one member of a party at some point along the way – it did to me on the Churchill in 1955, and to Pam on Lake Superior in 1960. When it does happen, the best remedy seems to be rest. Unless an extreme emergency dictates otherwise, it is better not

Illness

to battle on but to accept the situation and wait for Nature to put things right. Usually 24 hours' sleep does the trick. At this point we were fairly well on schedule, so we waited; we could not have made much headway in the wind in any case.

With Bill lying in his tent, and Pam attempting to brew him hot broth using caribou moss for fuel, Arch and I walked over the tundra to keep warm. Suddenly we realized that we were on the line of march of hundreds of caribou, in herds of three or four hundred. We reckoned we saw about two thousand in an hour. In the path of one oncoming herd, we lay down and waited, then stood up when they were almost upon us. They parted and streamed past us on both sides, so close that we could have touched them.

Caribou

Above the wind, we heard a plane, losing height to land on the lake a little way off shore from us. A man stepped onto the pontoon and waved. This must be Terk Bayly, a friend of Arch's, who had said he might be accompanying the Ontario minister of Lands and Forests on a northern swing. Arch and I grabbed a canoe and paddled out, leaving Pam pacing the shore, dreaming of titbits that they might have thought to bring. Alas, no titbits, not even staples. We chatted in the plane's cabin, but the minister seemed to be uncomprehending of our difficulties. He asked, rather deprecatingly, why we were just sitting around – why weren't we paddling? They took off and left us to the mercies of Aberdeen.

Windbound

In the persisting gale, Aberdeen Lake presented our greatest navigational problem. The lake was sixty miles long and fifteen broad. We finally became pinned down completely on this lake for five days, and in ten consecutive days attained only forty miles. What made us realize that progress was impossible, if not dangerous, was rounding one of the many small peninsulas hanging down from the north shore. On the western side of it, of course, we had a tail wind, but when we turned back into the north, it was all we could do to make any progress at all. The gale kept trying to turn us outward, across the lake. The ugly fact was that one might not reach the southern shore before being swamped by the big waves, in the icy water.

Though the north shore of the lake was lined with high ice banks, we caught sight of a flat-bottomed gully coming down to the water and affording some degree of shelter from the furious gale. We got our tents up and decided to wait there till the wind went down. The days were ticking by: we were beginning to give up hope of catching the weekly plane at Baker Lake, and would soon have to phase into emergency rations. It became a problem to decide how best to conserve energy. One could huddle in one's sleeping-bag, getting ever chillier and more lethargic, or else force oneself into a brisk walk, though almost feeling the benefit of the last meal being drained away with every step.

On the fourth night, around midnight, a motor-boat came by and stopped. It was Andy with his party. He had decided that the weather was so bad that he might as well pack up for the season, so he was on his way out to Baker Lake. All seven of us crowded into our little 5 × 7 foot tent while we brewed some tea and I wrote a note for Andy to take to the RCMP at Baker Lake, explaining our pin-down. We could not now hope to make this week's plane, I wrote, but would get out when we could. If, in the meantime, there were a plane passing our way with room for four passengers, we could leave our canoes to be brought out over the snow next winter. Mindful of the etiquette of northern hospitality, Pam doled out the last of our bannock to our visitors, signalling the rest of us to hold back. She was puzzled that, when passed the sugar jar, Andy murmured, 'I haven't seen any of that for a little while.' Their cabin had seemed well-provisioned. The explanation came only months later, in Ottawa. Apparently, when packing up to leave the cabin, Andy had said to his Inuit helper, 'I'll pack the scientific gear. You see to the food for the journey out.' At their first stop, he said, 'Well, where's lunch?' and his assistant grinned and waved a rifle. It was all he had brought.

On the fifth day at this spot, the sun began to shine fitfully. The sand was actually warm to sit on, but within minutes the cold of the permafrost below seeped through. And then at about noon we saw a solitary mosquito, as welcome as a dove with

A sandbank gave scant shelter from the gale on Aberdeen Lake

an olive-branch, giving evidence that the wind was abating. More or less just to be doing something, and without much hope of getting far, we set off again. The wind was still strong, and we only achieved a mile in the first hour. But then, miraculously, the wind really began to slacken, and we sensed that we did have a chance. We had 135 miles to go to Baker Lake, the plane left in three days, and there was still Schultz Lake to cross. The last fifty miles, however, should be fast going, down the Thelon gorge, if only we could get that far. We decided to give it a try. We should attempt to keep paddling till 11 tonight, I said, and get up at 4 next morning. It would be worth the all-out effort, and we had never been defeated before.

As we were emerging from Aberdeen Lake in the early evening we saw what seemed a chimera, or a mirage, for a boat with outboard motor was coming toward us. It turned out to be an RCMP patrol, which they make from time to time, but now they were particularly on the lookout for us. We learned afterwards that conditions were so bad at Baker Lake when the two men had left that their wives were worried to see them go, and indeed they had had a terrible time getting up the Schultz Rapids, only succeeding at the third attempt. It was an almost inexpressible delight to us to meet them. We could have made it alone, but after our helpless pin-down we felt almost as though we were being rescued.

The patrol consisted of Sergeant Art Deer and Special Constable Seteenak. They asked what they could best do to help us, and I told them of our determination to get through by paddling late.'Then we'll go ahead and set up camp for you,' said Art. 'Supper will be ready at 11.' What a fantastic break! We paddled on with more hope, but we were tiring by the time we finally spotted their tent, set up where we had agreed, near the entrance to Schultz Lake. We were, if not actually starving after our pin-down, certainly very hungry. (We found, on 'weighing in' at Baker Lake, that we had all lost considerable weight from the cold and the low rations. An English expedition, going down the Back River just north of us at the same time, lost even more weight than we.)

Faye, Art Deer's wife, had prepared many delights for dinner: especially good were some freshly baked rolls and butter. We introduced our hosts to our daiquiris. The hors d'oeuvres that night (Bill's turn to provide) were fried grasshoppers, which took a little explaining to Seteenak. Art confessed to nostalgic memories of smoked oyster. Pam dived into a pack and produced some. We began to think that some weird stories would get around the north about our style of provisioning. After the cold of the past ten days, the heat of the single burner in the Coleman stove was overpowering, and we could scarcely crawl to bed.

We rose early as planned and tackled Schultz Lake, another long piece of water like Aberdeen, but this time we had no problem with wind. Ahead of us lay the Schultz Rapids at the head of the Thelon gorge, and the dangerous experience of Art and Seteenak on the way up showed that they were bad at the present high water. We probably could have navigated them by hugging the right-hand bank; however, we decided prudently and on the Mounties' advice to portage to just below the steepest waves.

Now we had a glorious last fifty miles down the gorge. The water was fast, but where the waves in the middle looked too high, we slunk down close beside the bank. Finally we reached the corner where the river turns sharply into the lake, and then headed into the bay on which sat the small Inuit community. Word of our coming had preceded us, through the Mounties. Every Inuit, it seemed, was on hand, photographing the arrival of the first Canadian recreational canoeists to have crossed the full breadth of the Barren Lands. We had made it despite all – the last 135 miles in just over two days – and would still be able to take off on our originally scheduled flight next day.

Baker Lake back in 1962 was a village of tents, with only five houses, allocated to white officials – RCMP, DOT, etc. There was, of course, a Hudson's Bay post, there was a small hospital, and an impressive church. (Next time we were there, in 1968, there were no tents at all, but rows of houses and even streetlamps.) Inspector Stu McKim of the RCMP and his wife Virginia very kindly invited the Morses to stay that night at their house; and the Deers had done the same for the other pair. We were taken to visit the people who ran the place. 'You must meet Canon James,' said Virginia, 'but we mustn't go over there just yet. I've sent someone over to warn him you're coming. He is up on the church roof, repairing it, and he would hate you to see him without his dog-collar.' We waited until word came that he could receive us, and sat round his table while he sang familiar hymns from a book printed in Inuk. The nurses showed us round the hospital, even to the crawl space where the year's supplies had to be stored. It made the job of provisioning for only a month's canoeing seem a trivial task. We went up the hill to the cemetery, for the view and to look at the grave of Arthur Moffatt. The nurses said they had to go up from time to time to repair the graves, replacing the covering stones that the foxes had pulled away. We remembered that we had not yet visited the HBC factor. 'You'll have to hurry,' they said. 'He closes at 5:30.' We were back in civilization.

Through the
sub-Arctic Forest

'Whatever you do, don't try paddling the Snare Canyon –
either up or down,' declared Dr Charles Camsell. I used to run
into him occasionally at luncheon, and if he were alone I would
take the opportunity to glean from his memories of his wide
travels by canoe in the North. Born and bred there, he had
been head of the Geological Survey and later deputy minister of
Northern Affairs. His warnings were not to be taken lightly.
But yet the Snare River tempted me.

The Hanbury-Thelon trip had whetted our appetite for that
country, and after a summer on more southerly waters we yearned
for the high north again. The Snare formed part of an attractive-
looking route, starting in the uplands near Clinton-Colden Lake,
where we had set off down the Hanbury two years earlier, but
this time heading westward instead of east. The logistics were
good: we could fly in by charter from Yellowknife to Clinton-
Colden Lake again. We planned to go through the Thanakoie
Narrows to Aylmer Lake, then up the Lockhart and over the
divide to the Snare, finishing at Rae near the western end of Great
Slave Lake and only sixty miles by road from Yellowknife. From
our starting-point it was about 350 miles to Rae as the crow
flies, but much longer via the great arch made by the Snare –
possibly 500 miles in all. We would be in the Barrens for the first
part of the trip, but would have trees from Winter Lake onward.

The only remaining doubt we had was negotiating the Snare. We could find no record of anyone who had paddled the whole length of the river – only visits here and there along its course by government geologists or wildlife personnel. Probably on account of the canyon, Indians had forsaken the full course of the river, branching off down the Wecho instead. Both rumour and report of potential trouble focussed on two sections of the Snare. The first of these, from Jolly Lake down to Winter Lake, was reported to be shallow and rocky, involving much portaging. The second, of course, was the canyon, where the river drops 270 feet in four miles. We debated it over the winter. So many reports that we had received of problems on other rivers and lakes had turned out to be gross exaggerations. Moreover – and this was what drew us – it did look as though it might be possible to find a way of bypassing the canyon altogether, by a series of short overland hops between little lakes and small creeks. In the end the temptation of 'exploring' was too great for us, and we decided to go.

There remained the question of a crew. From the first, Angus Scott was keen to go. Recently appointed headmaster of Trinity College School at Port Hope, he would be a strong and congenial member of the party, with plenty of canoeing experience though none in the north or on long trips. But finding a fourth member of the crew baffled us. It seemed to be a year when all our best canoeing friends had family or professional commitments. The make-up of a canoe party has to be right, particularly with a small group of four, and in remote country. Suddenly we thought of Terk Bayly. Though none of us actually knew him, we had mutual friends, and I had met him briefly when he had landed by float-plane on Aberdeen Lake in 1962. A canoeist from boyhood, he was a professional forester and outdoorsman, and was at that time deputy minister of Lands and Forests for Ontario. We arranged what had become a traditional 'shake-down' trip in May up the Barron River in Algonquin Park and down the Petawawa. It was at once clear that we had a good team. Terk, never one to waste words, was a quick thinker and an expert doer. Pam would as usual be cook and be in charge of the commissariat. Angus nobly agreed to serve as assistant cook and proved to be an equable and innovative one.

We met our first serious problem early: it had been a late spring in the north and, as we flew in from Yellowknife, we looked down and discovered that Clinton-Colden Lake was locked in ice. Directing the pilot therefore to turn back westward along our intended route, we found Aylmer Lake also icebound, but to our relief the west wind had blown the long bay in its southwest corner free of ice, and there we landed, hoping that the wind would not change in the night and lock us in. Our pilot lost no time in heading for home. It was 11 pm – a glorious Arctic evening, with low sunlight. All around us lay the beautiful Barrens which on our first acquaintance had looked bleak and bare, but which we had come to love for their endless vistas, their clear air, their solitude, and the explosion of colour. 'There's some music coming from away over there,' said Terk, pointing. We listened; it sounded like a far-off choir. It could only be, we decided, the build-up of sound from ice-pans rubbing against each other and on distant rocks. We were alone, miles from anyone. The trip had now been shortened by the distance from Clinton-Colden, and we felt optimistic, though the possibility of solid ice ahead on big McKay Lake was a nagging worry. For the time being, however, we relaxed and savoured the luxuries of the first-night camp: steaks broiled on charcoal, washed down with burgundy. The ice-free bay of Aylmer Lake was the real start of our journey.

Discouragement hit us again next day, when a brisk headwind blew up. We struggled for two and a half hours along the shore of Aylmer Lake, in which time we made only five miles. It was pointless to battle on, and we could only hope for a lull towards evening. To distract ourselves from the frustration of sitting waiting, a fishing contest was arranged between Terk and Angus, the penalty for the loser being to find the wood to cook the winner's catch. Terk landed a monster lake trout within two minutes; it took Angus half an hour's hard work to find enough willow twigs to cook it. Clearly this exposed, sandy, fuelless beach was no place to camp, if we were pinned down for the night, so we moved to relative shelter in a little nick in the shore. It was no grand harbour, but in that country the tiniest windbreak is valuable. By the time we had had dinner, the wind had slackened marginally, and there was the familiar debate as to the need to push on. I am myself opposed to night paddling unless it is absolutely necessary. Better, I consider, to get a good night's sleep and to start off fresh and early next day than to struggle on, with the dreary prospect of making camp late, in the dark. In this instance, I was not convinced that the need was urgent or that the wind had dropped that much. But the majority were eager, so we gave it a try, teaming Pam with Terk to balance the muscle-power. We were soon forced to give up and return to our small 'haven' and the tiresome business of setting up the tents for the second time. Altogether a disappointing start.

The next day we were on our way by 8 am, with the wind now on our beam and not quite so strong, and we thankfully reached the foot of the bay on Aylmer Lake by noon. Terk and Angus had made a surprise detour toward the shore, convinced that some smallish black boulders were muskoxen. They were chagrined at their mistake — a dramatic illustration of the distortion one experiences when entering the Barren Lands, where the absence of trees causes problems in sizing things. We were surprised to find a loon's nest on the shore, even though the lake was not yet free of ice.

We had looked forward to the next stretch, up the Lockhart to Jolly Lake, as a change from lake travel. On the maps and air photos, the river had looked to be of manageable size. But it proved to be a tough struggle against a strong current, and an adverse wind besides. There were many more rapids than marked on the map, and those that were marked usually turned out to be falls. These we welcomed because they meant that we would be taking up the climb more quickly. Altogether we made ten portages on our way to McKay Lake, three of them about a mile long, and the ground was mostly poor for portaging, as is common in divide country. Probably at lower water-

level some of these portages could be avoided, but we were
still contending with the spring run-off.

Planning ahead for this upstream work, more particularly on
the smaller Snake River above McKay, we had ordered from
the Hudson's Bay Company in Yellowknife four stout ten-foot
poles, which we shod with iron ferrules supplied by Terk.
There had been poling practice on the Barron in the spring, and
now we put this to use. Terk based his style on that of the
Indians in the Winisk area, which involved both canoeists' poling at once, a procedure frowned on by Pam, who had learned
to pole on quiet English rivers, and preferred to do it solo, assis-
ted by crude steering from the bow paddler. However, even if
unaesthetic, the synchronized efforts of Terk and Angus, both
poling, were better able to cope with the fierce current and
tortuous course, although they were once detected turning in a
complete circle. And so, depending on the drop, we paddled,
poled, and portaged our way up.

On one of these portages, past a falls, Terk, who was double-
packing ahead, came upon a large Barren Grounds grizzly,
asleep under a willow-bush. He wanted to say quietly to Angus,
who was following with the canoe, 'Look out, there's a grizzly,'
but the words wouldn't come. At this point the bear awoke,
took one startled look at an aluminum canoe advancing on
two legs, and galloped towards the horizon like an express train.
At the top of a rise, it stopped and looked back, snorted, and
took off again.

This seems to be typical of the behaviour of Barren Grounds
grizzly on meeting humans, provided they have ample warning; on this occasion things were more tense since we had taken
the animal by surprise. People are often astonished that we do
not take firearms, but I consider that they may do more harm
than good, and they are not strictly legal up there in any case,
except for self-defence. We had decided, after our 1962 trip on
the Hanbury-Thelon, never again to take a gun. On the Kazan,
one of the party insisted on bringing fire-crackers for each of us,
the idea being to scare off unwelcome bears. Since the fire-

crackers were small and light the rest of us didn't object stren-
uously, though it did seem unlikely that one could, when
faced with an unfriendly bear, find time to dig out the crackers
and matches, and light the things.

There was plenty of other evidence of bear along the Lockhart.
Once we lunched on a sandy knoll which had been bulldozed
by grizzlies, swiping with their paws at the network of burrows
made by ground-squirrels, their favourite protein. Similar to
small marmots, these little creatures are called sik-sik by the
Inuit, because of their alarm note.

On its course down from McKay Lake, the Lockhart runs
through two small lakes, the Outrams. Here we were pinned
down for a day by gale-force winds, laced with rain and hail. The
photos bring back the misery of the place: the canoes propped
on their sides to give a little shelter for cooking and stores. It was
the last time we took a stove. In the cold and wind, so much
heat was lost from the little Optimus, before reaching the pot,
that Pam was unable even to cook the breakfast eggs. They
were almost raw, and were in addition rather high. Angus pro-
fessed not to care, and drank them while the rest of us
shuddered.

It was at this miserable campsite that Angus, a Seagram connection, produced his special treat – a bottle of 54-year-old
rye. He thought that this might be the low point of the trip.
Perhaps he was right. We were certainly concerned about the
delays, and even more about whether McKay Lake would be free
of ice. Terk had brought along some maps of the country
flanking our route, and we studied them for alternatives to
McKay, via smaller waters. There were some faint possibilities, but they would take us a long way off course.

Then the weather began to smile, and our spirits rose as we
forged ahead up the Lockhart. Eventually we emerged on
McKay Lake, finding to our joy that it was quite free of ice, and
that in fact we had a brisk tail-wind. Although weary from our
strenuous ascent of the Lockhart, we felt that the opportunity
was too good to miss: we should keep paddling and put big
McKay behind us, at any rate to a point where we would be out

of danger of another pin-down. We stopped part way for a
quick one-pot dinner, then set out again, this time all in agreement that night paddling was called for. The wind had died
completely, and we felt we could risk striking right across the
lake, even though the far shore could not be seen against the
low sun. Safe at last on the northwest shore, we set up camp, our
tents almost dwarfed by huge boulders reminiscent of Stone-
henge. Hot soup was welcome before bed at 12.30 am – it had
been a twenty-and-a-half hour day and strenuous work, mostly
upstream.

Our next problem was to make our way up the Snake River,
little more than a rocky, brawling brook, still in spring spate.
There could be no paddling, and even poling was difficult. We
waded most of the rapids, pulling our canoes; portaged some;
poled a few. In the hot, windless watercourse, the blackflies
were thick and aggressive: we were literally scraping layers of
them off our eyelids. Headnets were out of the question because
we needed to be able to see the rocks below the surface. On
the second day of this, we tried switching partners, Pam with
Terk again, to see if the better balance of muscle-power would
permit better poling. But it was not to be – we all had to wade.
Pam had made the mistake of thinking that her wading-days
were over for the time being, and had put on waterproof boots
instead of running shoes. 'One good thing about boots,' she
remarked to Terk as she clambered into the canoe for perhaps
the twentieth time, 'is that the water stays in them instead
of flooding the canoe.' 'A very British remark,' murmured
Terk.

An exceptionally high esker flanked our course, and we
crossed the small lake we were on to climb it and get the view.
Eskers are dominating features of the landscape in the Barrens:
inverted water-courses, they mark where rivers long ago flowed
beneath mile-deep glaciers. But instead of gouging a ditch in
the land, the river would build up its detritus of rocks and
sand along its winding course beneath the ice, and when the
glacier later melted a high ridge was left. Some eskers are a
hundred feet high or more. Relatively smooth on top, they have

been known to serve as routes for migrating caribou, and even as emergency landing strips for bush pilots.

At one campsite near the tree-line, we found a 'grove' of miniature spruce, no more than knee-high, spreading from root-stock and giving the impression of a miniature spruce forest looked at from a plane. And on Courageous Lake, which we came to soon, there were sizeable trees growing on the south-facing side of an esker. Here we had a camp that we called Grand View. I have always, over the years, mentally labelled the days by names characterizing the campsite. Angus, however, labelled them by notable events, such as 'The Day of the Grizzly'. This day, in his diary, was 'The Day the Cook Fell Over'. Regrettably, there was also, later, 'The Second Day the Cook Fell Over'. It was useless for Pam to protest that her mishaps were due to the uneven ground, not to the effect of a tot of rum after twenty-seven miles of slogging.

Continuing up out of Courageous, we found the river much more manageable, and were soon able to paddle again. We had here another demonstration of the tricks of heights and distances in the Barrens. Pam and I, nearing a portage, headed for where we had seen Terk on shore, waiting for us, we thought. We were a little surprised to find, on landing, that he had not stayed to help us, as all of us usually did for each other, but we buckled down to our loads. We were still more puzzled to find neither of them at the other end of the portage, and indeed the carry had been surprisingly short. It was not until we started on the return trek for our second load that we realized that there was water flowing on both sides of the portage — we had toiled across a small, low island! Terk, on the mainland behind the island, had looked so tall that the island in the foreground had failed to show, and we had begun our portage without even thinking of checking. The other two were by now gazing at us in astonishment from the further shore, wondering if we were really as bushed as we appeared to be, portaging unnecessarily over an island.

We reached Jolly Lake at last, the end of our uphill toil. There would be a short carry from the lake to the start of the Snare,

Atop an esker near the Snake River, above McKay Lake

then downhill all the way. To celebrate, we had freeze-dried raspberries with the bannock 'shortcake' for dessert. Terk's hors d'oeuvres that night had been rather startling: tiny black octopi, entire, with body and tentacles. I called them 'testicles' and spurned them. I discovered later that for the rest of the trip the other three, all of whom had brought the odd can of the more usual sort of octopus slices as their hors d'oeuvre contributions, had contrived to hoodwink me into thinking they were swordfish so that I would eat them.

By now we had no further use for our poles (we thought), so we sawed them up for firewood, to leave for anyone who might follow us. The next morning, determined not to be thwarted in our progress, we got up at 3 and were off before 5 to paddle the last sixteen miles to the west end of Jolly Lake. There a *boisson* of rum was shamelessly declared, before lunch at 9. We built a cairn to house the firewood, and also inserted a bottle with a paper saying who we were and when we had passed. We gave the name and address of our youngest member, Angus, for we were curious to know if there would ever be any other traffic on this route. No one wrote. Some ten years later a friend, Professor A.C. Hamilton of Queen's University, with his sons followed our route and reported that the cairn (like the one at Helen Falls on the Hanbury) lay demolished, but that they had made good use of the firewood. This strengthened my belief that Barren Grounds grizzlies have come to associate cairns with food caches and destroy them in their search for goodies.

The actual source of the Snare could be described as no more than a seepage area a few yards from where we had landed, and we had to portage three-quarters of a mile to reach enough depth of water to float a canoe. From this point down to Winter Lake, we watched the Snare grow from a streamlet to a sizeable river. Despite the hard work, there is something exciting about working down a river from its very start until it becomes a powerful flow. You develop a special bond with the river, and as you travel down you adjust to its increasing power and changing terrain. I remember this with particular pleasure for the Hanbury and the Coppermine. Here on the Snare, the going was

at first tough. Of the first thirteen miles we portaged four, for
only the little lakes were deep enough to take a canoe; their
connecting streams were not. At times we wished we had not
abandoned our poles. We wondered if the whole idea of taking
on the Snare had been crazy. A note of encouragement was
struck when we found a small paddle almost buried in the tundra, quite old, apparently whittled by an Indian for a child. A
little later we found a roll of birchbark, carried for repairs. Evidently other people had once really used this route. Then we
began to find more current, and rapids that could be run or
waded. Below the longest lake in this chain we had only three
portages and several runnable stretches. In all, getting down to
Winter Lake from Jolly took us three days: a day of toil, a day
of mostly paddling, and a day of fun, running, lining, and wading
rapids.

Shortly before reaching Winter Lake, Angus and Terk set out
with great panache from the foot of a waterfall to run a boiling
rapid. We followed more cautiously, wading for a short distance
first, then embarking on an exciting run. At the final rocky
apron, so typical of Arctic rivers, we found the others in the
water, with a swamped canoe. This went down in their record
as 'The Day the Wave Came In'. For myself, their mishap re-
sulted in a distinct benefit. Angus had brought along an anthol-
ogy of poetry, and every evening at the happy hour he would
declare 'The pome (his pronunciation) for tonight is ...' and
then declaim his selection for the night in sonorous tones. I
confessed to being happy to see that the poetry-book was one
of the casualties of their swamping. For days after this, Angus
would seize any opportunity to spread the wan pages out to
dry in the sun, until one glorious gust of wind blew the last
surviving pages away. My own mischievous riposte, I delivered later, at our reunion in Toronto to look at our slides of the
trip, when I inflicted on the party my own 'pome for tonight' –
a piece of doggerel recounting the events of the trip and repro-
duced at the end of this chapter.

Arrived at Winter Lake, we were keen to look nearby for the
remains of Sir John Franklin's Fort Enterprise, where he had

wintered in 1820 on his first trip to the Arctic. He had struggled
back there from the north the following October, half the
party having died of starvation on the way. But the site of Fort
Enterprise lay below the first rapid out of Winter Lake, and
first we had to make camp and dry out. The fort's remains would
have to wait until next day. A long sandy tree-lined beach near
the outlet offered good camping and drying-space. In fact, it had
been heavily used by Indians fairly recently; we also found an
Indian grave among the trees, fenced with small stakes.

Next day, the first order of business was to get over the
portage and try to locate Fort Enterprise. I reckoned we could
spare a couple of hours for looking at what remained of the
fort. First, on the left bank of the river, below the portage, we
identified the spot from which George Back must have made
his sketch of Fort Enterprise. Then we crossed the river and
looked around. The site was extraordinarily elusive. It wasn't
in any of the places one would have expected, nor could we
discover it from the contemporary narratives and sketches
which we had with us. The search was made more difficult by
the litter of two or three Indian campsites, with drying racks.
It seemed ridiculous to be there, armed with such full descriptions, and not be able to find the spot, but eventually we had
to give up, so as to keep on schedule. We felt consoled when we
heard, on our return to Ottawa, from a retired government
surveyor. From a base camp near ours, in 1938 he had spent
several evenings vainly searching for the fort and succeeded
only when he chanced to follow his dog into the willows, where
it had been chasing some small animal. He had erected a
wooden marker there, beside the rotting remains of the wooden
foundations, but by the time we came the willows must have
grown up to mask the place. This must all seem extraordinary
now, since the site has doubtless become very obvious after
several seasons of archeological 'digs'.

We saw our first robin here, and our first caribou as we entered
Roundrock Lake after two more rapids. The going was now
easy, through Roundrock and Snare lakes, both large. There was
a forest fire on the south shore of Snare Lake, and what looked

to be a more serious fire down the Wecho River. We were thankful that we had decided against taking the Wecho route. Near the foot of Snare Lake we had a surprise, for there was a sudden and unadvertised drop of about ten feet through some rocky rapids, though the two sections of the lake above and below the rapid were both clearly marked on the map with exactly the same altitude. An eagle was sighted at these rapids. The Snare River was now starting to break off through fast passages to the north, for we were approaching the canyon and our most critical exploration was about to begin. We avoided the main exit of the Snare, below which the river plunges through rapids leading to the gorge itself, and our task now was to probe north or west to find a way to get back on the Snare again, preferably at a point below its canyon.

Since time and energy were at a premium, we planned our reconnaissance like a military operation. First we landed on a steep-sided, rocky little island, close to our jump-off area, and deposited our eight packs there, as a precaution against bears; then we split up into two separate parties. From studying the map and air photos, I favoured a route from a tiny bay, heading for two small lakes in line with our general direction. Other little lakes were stretched out beyond these, and with luck we could portage and puddle-hop to below the canyon. But first there were two flanking routes to be checked, one on either side. Terk and Pam took on the more easterly scouting, which consisted of working down a small creek to hit the Snare just above the canyon, and then assessing the possibility of getting down it somehow. Angus and I undertook the more westerly reconnaissance, looking for a portage from the foot of the long bay of Snare Lake. We soon gave that up as hopeless, and came back to attack the more central route, from the little bay. To our delight, it seemed to be fairly good. We portaged and paddled via the first two little lakes, then came upon the other canoe, parked where Terk and Pam had evidently decided to go on by foot towards the head of the canyon. We scribbled a note on a scrap of paper, telling them of our discoveries, and saying we planned to prospect the way ahead towards the canyon's foot.

The air photos made it quite clear where we were. From where Terk and Pam had left their canoe, we needed to portage only fifty yards to reach the next lake, after which a short carry would take us to another small lake, from whose steep shore rose a ridge that separated us from the canyon of the Snare. Once on top of this ridge, we would only have to portage the short stretches between three more small lakes to reach a point where we should be able to look down on the Snare as it emerged from the canyon. There was no portage path, but the spruce trees of the northern forest were widely spaced, making it easy to pick our course. Angus and I went just far enough to satisfy ourselves that we would be able to get through next day, and then returned to look for the other two.

Pam and Terk, meantime, had struggled down the creek through sketchy water, then bushwacked through to a view of the canyon. The tributary stream would, they felt, provide a marginally feasible route to the Snare, although it would involve a long portage and some dicey rapid-running. From there, the Snare itself and its canyon could be attempted, but only as a last resort. Returning sombrely, they were overjoyed to find our optimistic note, and swung into action. Our message was marked 3 pm, so they guessed we would be late back, and tired. They took the route that we had found, back to Snare Lake, fetched the packs from the island, and set up the tents on the mainland shore at the start of the portage. Terk wisely then walked back along the portage, to leave us a note that there was no need to carry our canoe all the way back to Snare Lake. He met us just crossing the last little lake, still with good news. The way ahead, we said, looked feasible, and the country was fairly open. It was a happy camp that night: we felt we had handled the operation effectively, and we looked forward to working our way around the canyon and over to the Snare next day.

We were up early to attack the portages, and were away by 7, making quick progress through the first few little lakes, thanks to the preliminary scouting of the day before and good teamwork on the portages. It proved to be a steep climb to the top of the ridge flanking the canyon, but after that the going was good, and we made eight portages in all before stopping for lunch. The day was hot and the blackflies were bad, but we didn't seem to care now. Angus has a habit of declaiming poetry as he portages, especially when the going is tough. His voice would boom from under the canoe, 'Say not the struggle naught availeth,' or something similarly inspirational. This would often be interrupted by an explosion of snorts as he tried to spit out the flies that had invaded his open mouth.

Eventually we had the joy of sighting the Snare down below us, broad and welcoming. That last long portage down the big descent was the worst, through six-foot willows and birches, which made it difficult to keep contact and all hold to the same direction. We resorted to using our whistles. However, we achieved a perfect 'landfall' and were water-borne on the Snare again by noon.

Entering Indin Lake, we saw a large white tent and were hailed by two prospectors, brothers grubstaked from Toronto. Their camp was spotless, and so were they, clean-shaven and spruce, although they'd been in there since mid-May. We felt a little embarrassed at our less immaculate appearance after only two or three weeks. They told us they had been coming in for twenty-three years. No doubt, in those circumstances it becomes important to maintain one's standards. Things were less rugged, they said, than they used to be: nowadays, they were reprovisioned by plane, every fortnight. They made us coffee, showed us a bear they had just killed, and — to our delight — made us a generous gift of a dozen fresh oranges. They were the only people we had met since leaving Yellowknife.

Indin Lake, twenty-eight miles long, is one of the most beautiful we have seen, with high granite points and many rocky islands. The shores were parklike, the well-spaced trees set in carpets of yellow lichen and moss. It was hot; we were all tired from our five-hour portage the day before, and swam often. Nevertheless, we kept up a good pace and made good mileage, as we had to do if we were to get through on schedule. A brisk headwind arose, occasionally whipping up the surface into a whirling, dancing dervish that spun across the lake.

The Snare in its lower reaches, grown from a trickle to a majestic river

At the foot of the lake, we ran into more difficulty, for the
Snare had become a narrow granite-bound river, descending a
steep valley with sharp drops and cataracts, most of which we
had to portage. There were a few signs of old cuttings, but the
path was mostly overgrown and trees continually blocked the
way, especially for portaging canoes. We were told later of two
young Americans who had just come to grief near here. They
had chartered in to Indin Lake. In the fast water at the lip of a
drop, their canoe's outboard motor had failed. They had both
leaned over at the same moment to grab a bush, the canoe had
flipped and was carried away, leaving them stranded and without food, without boat, tent, or gear. Fortunately they were
spotted by a plane and rescued after a few days, hungry and
nearly demented from insect bites. They were lucky – a
simple mishap like this, for a one-canoe party, can be disastrous
in that part of the country.

We finished this stretch by running some enjoyable rapids and
fast water, realizing sadly that these were the last, for we had
now entered large Bigspruce Lake, the headpond behind the
Snare Dam. By now we were really pushing hard, to reach the
dam at the foot of the lake and send a message to the RCMP
confirming our expected time of rendezvous with them on
Slemon Lake the day after next. On our way in, the Yellowknife
RCMP detachment had insisted on having a boat from Rae
meet us at the end of the portage into Slemon Lake. We had
protested our wish to be independent, but they were adamant,
and we got the idea that perhaps the Rae detachment would not
want to be done out of a little break from routine. Certainly it
was good not to be faced with paddling two long lakes at the end
of the trip, with the possibility of an adverse wind. So we had
said that on that day we would be at the end of the portage into
Slemon at 9 am, and that we would confirm by phone from
the dam. We felt we should try to phone before nightfall, even
though it meant a forty-mile day.

The dam itself was slightly off our course, and we camped two
miles from it, Pam and I setting up camp while the other two
paddled off to the dam to send the message. We had only got one

Angus Scott catching up on sleep and waiting for the Mounties on Slemon Lake

tent up before we heard a motor-boat, and there they were, being towed back by the dam-keeper and his wife, who had broadmindedly abandoned their plans for a fishing trip and a shore supper, to come and picnic with us. Edie Tench's first remark on seeing Pam was, 'You know, you could have had a bath at our place.' We did not let her forget this. The Tenches generously gave us cookies and fruit including, notably, strawberries from their freezer. We were really coming close to civilization!

Below the dam, the Snare is again unfriendly to canoeists, with bad canyons and falls. We chose instead to take the old Indian canoe route to Slemon, using an attractive chain of small lakes leading south from the long south bay of Bigspruce Lake. There were fifteen portages in all, more than expected, and not much used, since most of the traffic goes by the winter road over the muskeg, close to the river. Eventually we took to the tractor-trails ourselves, which were messy but had firmer footing.

And so finally we were camped below a hill at the start of the last portage, poised to make our meeting at 9 next day. I have always been something of a stickler for punctuality. In 1966 on the Coppermine, there was general amusement when I told the RCMP that we expected, after three weeks' canoeing, to arrive at Coppermine itself on a certain day by 5.30 pm. To their astonishment, we indeed arrived on that very day, at 5.15. In the present instance, we all felt it incumbent on us to be at our rendezvous on time, and we streamlined our gear, the food packs now slender, so that we could do the two-mile portage in one carry – one person with the canoe and a lightish pack, the other with two heavier packs. We were over by 8.30, but our wait was a long one. We made a smudge fire against mosquitoes, and most of us slept. Pam was just beginning, mournfully, to wonder what to cook for supper, when the boat came in sight – apparently the police had lost their way. We rejoiced, on the ride down to Rae, through Slemon, Russell, and Marian lakes, that we had not had to battle in a canoe the strong headwind down these fair-sized lakes.There was a welcoming group at Rae, at that time a very small community. The village itself centred on just a few houses perched on a sheet of smooth rock. Corporal Palliser of the RCMP insisted, despite our protests, on our having dinner with the family: another example of the fabled northern hospitality, for they already had his in-laws from Missouri staying with them. Moreover we, who were flying home tomorrow, were made to share the goodies that these visitors had brought up from the south – fresh fruit and vegetables unprocurable at Rae. All we could offer in return was our overproof rum, and as an hors d'oeuvre – of course – 'swordfish'.

Finally, later that evening, replete and content, we bundled with our packs into a truck for the bumpy ride to Yellowknife. Angus was asleep in seconds. For the rest of us, the unfamiliarity of a dark evening sky, and even stars, brought home the fact that we had been in another world. The trip has remained in memory as one of the best, nearly five hundred miles with a good crew, varied and scenic country, and the added fillip of exploring our way.

The 'pome for tonight'
inflicted on our dinner-gathering in Toronto:
my riposte to Angus' poems at the happy hour.

In the Steps of Hiawatha
(By an obscure poet)

In the land of Hearne and Franklin,
In the moon when loons are nesting,
Aylmer Lake was locked in pack ice;
Clinton-Colden too was covered.
Naught to do but turn in mid-air,
Have the big-bird change direction,
Drop the paddlers on the Barrens,
But beyond the wintry prospect,
On a point in clouds of insects.

Little time was lost unloading,
Fire built and willow gathered.
Terk then tethered tents, while Angus,
Sitting cross-legged like a pixie,
Muttering foggy incantations,
Conjured up a brew ambrosial.
Meanwhile Pamela on charcoal
Grilled thick steaks, because the party
For a moon would know privation,
Suffer hardship, sense starvation:
Dehydrated stuff and corned beef
(Every second day more corned beef);
Now and then a blackened bannock,
Octopus and other horrors,
In a tent with clouds of insects.

High above, in silent anger,
Kitchimanitou was watching,

Viewed the four invading Paleface,
Saw them paddling on the Barrens,
In the land that he'd forbidden
To the Eskimo and Indian.
First he threw a west wind at them,
While they huddled in a harbour.
Then he brewed a mighty North Wind.
Laced with rain and gale and hailstones.
But the voyageurs, undaunted,
Pitched their tents beneath a cutbank,
Quaffing Seagram's best distilling,
In the mud in clouds of insects.

Then the Manitou, relenting,
Changed the order of the seasons;
Sent the sun to shine and bake them;
Made the wind a gentle maiden,
Not the harridan she first was;
Strewed the Barren Lands with flowers;
Caused the grizzly bear to gallop;
Kept the cook from falling over.
Cheered once more, the four proceeded,
Poling up the roaring rapids,
Paddling peacefully and quickly;
Many portages through muskeg,
Through great swamps with clouds of insects.

After twenty days of toiling,
Waning with the moon above them,
Now the voyageurs a shadow
Of themselves before they started,
O'er a mighty ridge they carried,
Through to Slemon Lake they portaged.

Here it was the mounties found them,
Looking sleepy, gaunt and haggard;
Looking forward to a bath-tub,
To a cloistered nook with plumbing,
Not a vulnerable posture
On a hill with clouds of insects.

Blocked on the Kazan

The Kazan was next on our program of Arctic rivers, but after
our long pin-down on Lake Aberdeen in 1962 we were reluctant
to start near its very source, close to the NWT boundary, for
this would involve traversing two big lakes, Ennadai and Kasba.
Our plan in 1968 was to fly to Stony Rapids at the eastern end
of Lake Athabasca and there charter a plane to take us part way
down the Dubawnt River, to a point where we could start
with some good river running and soon pick up a stream flowing
over to the Kazan, joining it below its big lakes. Such a stream
was the Kamilukuak, flowing from near Carey Lake on the
Dubawnt River. The Dubawnt flows out of Wholdaia Lake and into
Beverly Lake on the Thelon; the Kazan lies east of the Dubawnt
and runs parallel to it, ending up at Baker Lake, at the western
end of Chesterfield Inlet. The whole trip would be about four
hundred miles. Our party, besides Angus, Bill Mathers, and our
two selves, consisted of some newcomers: Pat Baird, Peter
Blaikie, Ernie Howard, and Tom Lawson.

Our plane descended to Stony Rapids through banks of cloud,
and the rain began as we unloaded, an inauspicious start to
what turned out to be a trouble-plagued trip from start to finish.
As we went about our tasks in the little settlement – collect-
ing our canoes and supplies from the Hudson's Bay Company,
repacking the groceries, giving the RCMP our schedule, and

obtaining fishing licences – the rain settled in. The afternoon dragged on, and we had anxious conferences with our charter pilot, a quiet middle-aged man who was clearly not going to be hustled into flying under risky conditions. We respected his caution. He had only the one plane, and with eight in our party, he would have to make a double trip. The flight itself would not be long, but the poor visibility and impending darkness were factors to reckon with. The HBC factor turned over to us an empty warehouse, where we stored our packs, out of the rain. As the hours ticked away, our frustration mounted.

Finally there came a temporary lull in the rain, and we had to make a hard decision. The pilot, somewhat reluctantly, was prepared to fly at least half the party but warned that, if conditions worsened again, he could not undertake to make the second trip that evening. This would mean splitting the party, and who knew for how long? It is never a good idea to separate in remote country. On the other hand, the first group could start paddling in fairly narrow, fast water, and as long as they went no further than the start of Carey Lake, the second group could be reasonably certain of spotting them from the air, to reunite the party. It might be days before we had good enough weather for two consecutive flights. We decided to take the risk of splitting up, and some hasty repacking was done to make sure that each group would be self-sufficient. Having made the offer, the pilot was anxious to be away. We agreed that the four to go ahead should be the youngest, and keenest for whitewater, so the choice fell on Angus (to be leader), Peter, Bill, and Tom.

With typical northern hospitality, Millie Goddard, the factor's wife, insisted that the remaining four of us should join them for dinner. This kindness brought a note of cheer to an otherwise depressing evening. The rain became a downpour, and we fully expected to see the rest of the party return. But no, the pilot came back alone, reporting that he had landed them, somewhat unceremoniously, on the shore of Boyd Lake, as planned. We heard later that they did no more than scramble into tents in the deluge, and attempt to drown their sorrows. At this point they found, as Pam had already realized to her horror, that they had been provided with no rum. Fortunately, Angus' now-traditional bottle of well-aged Seagram's rye was at hand, never more appreciated.

I will not dwell on the next thirty-six hours. The Goddards were tireless hosts, but we, the remaining four, were already embarrassed at being on their hands and were impatient to be away. The low cloud persisted. We slept in the warehouse among our packs that night, anxious to leave the Goddards in peace, and with an arrangement to fly very early next morning if possible. The pilot looked dubious as we took off, and when we reached the first range of hills and found them heavily banked in cloud, he muttered and turned the plane back toward home. We wondered what Millie would say when her unbidden guests turned up on her doorstep yet again. But there was Ray Goddard at the dock, announcing cheerfully, 'Millie's got the pancakes cooking. Come along to breakfast.' Another example of northern hospitality.

Finally, late in the afternoon, the sun came out, and we flew north. As we passed Boyd Lake and followed the course of the Dubawnt down to Barlow Lake, all eyes were on the lookout for the others. But we saw no sign. It was not safe to put down beyond the start of the next lake, Carey, for that had been our agreement, and beyond this point we could miss each other for days. It was certainly puzzling, in fact worrying – could there have been a misunderstanding? The pilot, after dropping us, made a quick circuit further on down Carey Lake for us, just in case, but without finding them.

Next morning, still rather disquieted with half the party missing, the four of us set off after breakfast to walk back upstream, along the bank of the Dubawnt, thinking we would make faster progress on foot than toiling up the rapids and riffs, and expecting to meet the other four at any moment. But we went further and further, and still no sign. It was a joyous moment when suddenly two canoes shot round a bend ahead of us. They landed in an eddy, and there was an exuberant reunion. Apparently, they had indeed been setting up camp on Barlow Lake when we flew over. Even though we had been strain-

ing to spot them, their overturned canoes had failed to catch our
eyes, perhaps because of the low evening sun. Realizing this,
they had pushed out on the lake in one canoe, but by then it was
too late. The 17-foot Grumman canoes were now tested to
their limit as we all eight piled into the two canoes and ran the
rapids back to our camp with barely two inches' freeboard.

The change in our fortunes put us in good spirits, and most of
us were even able to enjoy the task of working our way over
from Carey Lake, eastward, portaging over the tundra to where
we could put into the Kamilukuak River. This would eventually lead us, paddling and portaging, to the Kazan River, flowing northward. The blackflies were fierce, and some of the
small lakes were too shallow to paddle, but it was so good to be
all together and on our way, almost on schedule, that we did
not care. The few in the party who had had no recent opportunity to practise portaging were feeling it a little. We were
amused by Pat's insistence on building cairns along any portage
of more than trivial length. For the rest of us, it seemed enough
to do as we usually did, marking the route only temporarily by
sticking up inverted paddles, for we should never be seeing
those portages again. But Pat was a moutaineer, and to him
building cairns was a sacred duty. Every man has his own priori-
ties. Pat, a true Arctic expert who climbed on Baffin Island every
year, had never canoed before. He confided later, in Ottawa,
that he had come along partly to see if he could change his
attitude toward rivers. On Baffin, a river was an enemy, an
obstacle to progress, having to be forded with danger and discomfort, whereas on a canoe trip a river was a highway, a
welcome and usually pleasant means of progress. He stoically
hid his dislike of rivers, during the trip, but it proved
unshakable.

We had some attractive campsites along this stretch. A particularly memorable one was on a ridge partway across the portage into Big Rocky Lake. In both directions, the view was spectacular, particularly of the quartz-strewn lake ahead, whose
waters shone a vivid blue in the clear light. Far off we saw what
looked like towering cliffs of ice, which we decided must be

some sort of mirage. Another notable camp was on a low rocky point, just before meeting the river. There were signs that this was a place once much used by the migrating caribou to cross the water. Crossing-places were few in this region of large lakes, and this was just the sort of spot they would choose: a low rocky shore, with deep, narrow water to swim across. At such a place, too, the Inuit would lurk at the right season, waiting to make a killing. Since they usually couldn't eat at once all they killed, a caribou crossing often had a meat cache nearby, and there was an ideal one here, a shallow cave, entered from above, with a cold stream flowing close by to aid refrigeration. The meat cache was a hole about six feet deep in the rock. Peering down between the rocks that formed a cover, we could just make out a human skeleton stretched out on the floor of the cavern, for the cache had become a grave, possibly for one of Farley Mowat's 'People of the Deer', who had years ago been forced to abandon this part of the north when the caribou either went elsewhere or were killed off.

After Big Rocky Lake, our river was deep enough to give us good rapid-running all the way down to the west end of Kamilukuak Lake. But at its last rapid, it plunged us straight into winter, though the date was only mid-July. All around us was snow and ice. The lake itself was covered by broken ice, with a few leads of water here and there between the flocs. Huge piles of ice, driven up by pressure, had built up on all the shoals and small islands. Extending along the northern shore were white cliffs of ice and snow, a close-up of what we had glimpsed on our way over from Carey. In fact, 80 per cent of the surface of Kamilukuak was clogged with pack ice for as far as we could see, down to the east end of the lake, where our course lay. We should have to find a way through this considerable obstacle.

Climbing the nearest ice-pile, to assess the possibilities, we could see what looked to be a broad lead of open water close to the south shore, but we would first have to work over to it. The narrow leads at hand gave just enough passage for us to force the Grummans through, but the canoes took a beating. Every so often the lead would narrow to grip the canoe like a vice, and

Ice on Lake Kamilukuak:

right Shirtless despite the ice-floes;

left Peter Blaikie descending a pile of ice-blocks,
after scouting the way ahead

there was nothing for it but to back out and seek another way. Sometimes we tried getting partly out of the canoe and dragging, but the ice was only marginally able to support a person's weight, and there were some near-catastrophes. The leads had an annoying habit of trending in the wrong direction for us, away from that precious channel near the shore. Peter's six-foot-five height came in useful as he frequently stood up in the canoe and surveyed the scene ahead to decide where to steer for next. Often, though, he would boom, 'There's *no* way!' When we seemed sometimes to be getting seriously separated from our objective, we would climb one of the ice-piles and revise our course.

Despite these problems, that morning remains in memory as a highlight of arctic travel. The whole scene was arrestingly beautiful with the ice floes white against the still, dark blue water, under a dazzling sky. Each ice-pile was a thing of beauty — huge slabs of ice, deep blue as one looked down into their depths, almost like an iceberg. We had a feeling of euphoria, for the situation was almost unreal. Most of us were shirtless in the hot sun, and there were no bugs. The ice fragments tinkled as they jostled against the canoes, prompting Peter to reach for his tape-machine to record this sound so nostalgically reminiscent of shaking a martini.

The east end of Kamilukuak, which we finally reached, was blocked by a narrow isthmus only half a mile wide separating Kamilukuak water from the next lake, Nowleye. There was evidence that the caribou had used the isthmus in their migrations. A stream flowed across the isthmus, down the five-foot difference in height between the two lakes, though our map indicated that at the time when the air photo was taken, in summer, no water connected them. At this time of year, despite the wintry surroundings, the water coming down from Nowleye represented spring flow. Putting on canvas running shoes we hauled the canoes up by hand, wading in the short stream, and launched again on Nowleye. But to our joy and amazement we beheld this lake to reveal an apparent freak in local climate, for Nowleye was almost entirely free of ice, while half a mile away lay a lake almost totally icebound. We enjoyed the freedom of paddling again. But the reason for the contrast between these two lakes, so close together, one frozen and one clear, dawned on us only when we returned home and did a little more research.

The difference in the surface of the two lakes was explainable, we speculated, only by the presence of Dubawnt Lake, a huge body of water lying, ice-bound, scarcely twenty miles from Kamilukuak, which unlike Nowleye lay due south of Dubawnt Lake, exactly in the direction of the prevailing winter gales. The influence of vast Dubawnt Lake, fifty miles in diameter, is in fact betrayed in its very name, which means 'frozen in summer'. The phenomenon is even on record in our short Arctic history. J.W. Tyrrell, travelling with his brother, J.B. Tyrrell, on their celebrated trip of exploration down the Dubawnt and Thelon to Hudson Bay in 1893, looked down on this scene from a hill north of Carey Lake. J.W. Tyrrell in his *Across the Sub-Arctics of Canada*, published in 1908, wrote: 'During the afternoon, as my brother was tramping in the interior, he reached the summit of an adjacent hill, where a most dreary and chilling scene opened to his vision. To the east and northward, not many miles away, and extending as far as the eye could reach, there appeared a vast white plain shrouded in drifting clouds of mist. It was evidently a great lake, still covered in the month of August with a field of ice, and was probably the Dubawnt or Tobaunt Lake, known in a lengendary way to the Athabasca Indians, and sighted over a hundred years ago by Samuel Hearne when on his journey to the Coppermine River.'

Some pleasant rapids out of Nowleye brought us to the Kazan itself, and so to Angikuni Lake. The wind from the north was picking up, so we crept along the north shore of the lake, in cold driving rain, and had to go a little way down the outlet before we could find a sheltered place to camp, on a beach protected by a high cutbank. We were wet and chilled. So many of our afternoons and evenings, it seemed, had been rainy and cold. The eastern arctic is more subject than the west to the influence of Hudson Bay, and we appeared to be getting even more

than our fair share of poor weather. Tom had earlier declared
that this was to be 'Talent Night', but it was generally agreed (to
the relief of some of us) that conditions were too miserable.
After supper it brightened into a superb evening, and climbing
the cliff above our camp we were rewarded by a stunning view
back over Angikuni, adorned by a huge rainbow. There on top
were signs of several burial-places, including one elaborate
grave with a cairn, and dog-harness complete with bells.
Another had a tall pole, and great pieces of a heavy stove. Were
these, we wondered, there because they were the proudest pos-
sessions of the deceased?

Next morning was still warm and sunny, and since we had, by
great perseverance, maintained our schedule despite all, I
thought it wise to declare a leisurely get-away, to give time to
dry out our gear and get reorganized. So we set out at 10.30, on
the start of several days of good running down the fast Kazan, a
considerable river by now. The water-level was high, perhaps
two feet higher than other accounts had suggested. Sometimes
this made the rapids easier to negotiate; sometimes the increased turbulence was almost unmanageable, and when the
course turned toward the north the headwinds made the going
tough. There were some portages to be made, one of them past a
spectacular falls. At one short portage, Peter, an expert whitewater canoeist, ran two of the canoes empty down a chute; at
another, Bill Mathers joined him in running two empty canoes.
Our 'happy hour' daiquiris were more than once embellished
with ice collected along the way. Despite the wind, we made
good progress down to Yathkyed Lake, so large that we had
feared being icebound again. Here, miraculously, the wind
dropped after lunch, encouraging us to attempt the long traverse
to the big peninsula halfway along our course, rather than
sticking to our original plan of hugging the north shore for
shelter. We just made it in time – eight miles in one and a half
hours – impeded only at the end by a sharp northwest wind on
our beam.

At the point of the peninsula we watched a white Arctic fox
that was eying two sandhill cranes. He was in full view, and

Lining down a rapid on the Kazan

appeared unperturbed by our presence, merely curious. It turned
out that he was the only wild animal we encountered on the
whole Kazan trip. We debated here whether to battle the wind
across the next traverse, or whether to make camp and bank
on less wind next day to get past Yathkyed. The weather seemed
to be generally improving at last – this was the first evening
without rain for days and the sky looked good – and some of the
party were very tired. So we decided to camp, a delay we had
reason to regret eventually.

It was in fact a beautiful evening. The fishermen were in luck,
but we had to dip into our reserve of firewood, for there was
not a vestige of wood around, not even willow twigs. Here Tom
provided us with one of our most hilarious incidents. Ever
hyperactive and hyper-enthusiastic, he established himself on a
large ice-platform attached to the shore to clean his monster
fish, happily hacking and scraping away, all the time explaining
to us that this was the most splendid place to do the job: 'See?
Clean and cold! All the blood runs down into the snow! Water
right at hand! Did you ever see such a trout?' What he did not
realize, while we were splitting our sides with suppressed laughter, was that the platform he was on had become detached
from the shore, and that he and his fish were floating away. His
dismay when he realized his predicament was funnier still.
Eventually we rescued him by canoe.

It was a good site for walking – flat and dry. After the rest of us
were in bed, we could hear Peter as he strode over the tundra,
tape recorder in hand, recording his impressions of this, his first
Arctic trip. He was evidently highly organized and highly
motivated, and yet able to accept philosophically the reverses
that beset us instead of getting impatient. Back in Montreal,
he not only carried a full load of legal work but was also giving
no less than three different evening courses of lectures a week
at Sir George Williams College. 'I like to push myself, to see if I
can do it,' he said.

In the small hours of the morning, our hopes were dashed by
the flapping of the tent, under the onslaught of a revived and
strong NNW wind. We had planned to get off early, and were up

at 4.40, but in vain: the wind was even stronger and we were pinned down for the day. Eventually we were able to make our way along the north shore, and finally escaped from Yathkyed by portaging across the tundra at the base of the peninsula at the lake's north-east end, rather than being forced out into the windswept main body of the lake.

Launching again after the portage, we were back in the main flow of the Kazan, and ran for miles of very fast water, dropping twelve feet per mile. The strong headwinds, however, made it tiring and confusing, for the course was broken by ledges and islands. After a hard pull across a bay, we decided to sit it out in hopes of a lull later. Angus reported that Pat, his canoe-partner, was getting pretty tired. It emerged after the trip that he had burst some blood vessels in his arms with the strenuous and unpractised paddling against such winds. Although it was only mid-morning, we put up the tents for shelter, and tried to conserve our strength by resting. Such times of pin-down are usually trying on the nerves, and tiring. Tents have to be put up, taken down again at the hint of a lull, and then put up again; meals are planned, then replaced by quick snacks, so as to be ready for a quick getaway. Everyone is on edge, and judgement can be warped in the desire to make progress.

On this occasion we optimistically planned an early supper, hoping for an evening lull as so often happened. We even got the tents down and all the gear packed up, but were forced to accept that the wind was still too strong. Our next hope was an early morning lull, so it was early to bed, with plans to be up at 3 am. We had (most of us) just got to sleep, some with sleeping-pills, when Tom and Peter raised a shout that the wind was down and we could be on our way. It was about 9 pm and already becoming dusk. The 'lull' was far from convincing, but the majority were for pressing on, so we forced ourselves into action again, cold and sleepy. Almost as soon as we set off, the head-wind freshened again, and we were toiling. By 11 it was darker than usual for an Arctic night. Suddenly we heard the noise of rapids ahead, unadvertised by the map. Peter and Tom, who were in the lead, landed to scout the rapids, while the rest of us held back for their report. They shouted that it was just a ledge, and that we could get round the outside, and down they started, the rest following. But we began to suspect that worse was to come, and having no wish to run blind we turned back upstream, with a strenuous struggle to cross-ferry to the shore, in the strong current above the ledge. It was too late for Peter and Tom to turn back, and in fact they managed to get through all right. They walked back to us to tell us what to expect, but by now we were too close to the lip to get into a good position for running, unless we first lined back upstream for some distance. So we settled for lining down the rapid, an unpleasant, slippery business in the dark. This was all getting too dangerous to be sensible, and when we huddled below the rapid to discuss what next to do, we agreed on a compromise: we would continue until either we came to another rapid (which, in the dark, we would not attempt to run or to line) or the wind became too strong.

It was the wind that stopped us, a few miles further down. To the misery of making camp in the dark was added the difficulty of finding a tent-site. On scouting back from the shore for a suitable place, we discovered that the ground was soaking wet, with warning patches of bog cotton all around. The shallow depression we had sought for protection from the wind was itself attracting a small rill of water, for it was raining now. No tent-sites were found there, and we had to climb a rise to where a row of big boulders offered a certain degree of shelter from the strong wind. In fact we discovered next morning that we had camped at another Inuit meat cache among the rocks, and that where we had landed there was another caribou crossing, in the narrows entering the lake. The wind rose to nearly gale force, and once again we found ourselves in insufficient shelter. We launched again and battled the wind and waves, but discovered we were only making a mile an hour.

We were now in Forde Lake, of only moderate size, fourteen miles long, but unfortunately our course still lay due north into the teeth of what by now was clearly a polar gale. The canoes were shipping water, and Pat, in particular, was in no shape to continue the struggle much longer. A tough, lean man, earlier he had commanded the Canadian Army's Exercise Muskox, crossing in winter with military vehicles the full width of the Barrens, from Hudson Bay to Yellowknife. He knew every plant, mushroom, animal, and bird. He was a great walker, but had never been in the position of having to use his arms for locomotion. It was something quite unforeseen to have Pat Baird a brake on the wheel of progress. If we could just get to the end of Forde Lake, we would be in narrower waters and fast current. But we were making so little headway that it seemed best to camp and hope that the gale would decrease in force – provided that we could find shelter anywhere. The low shores offered little windbreak, but eventually we spotted a small sandy point that would serve, with a nearby willow grove whose low bushes offered a doubtful degree of wind shelter. We landed and pitched tents among the willows, while the gale whistled and screamed, and the angry lake's high waves slapped the shore. We laughed grimly at the irony of being pinned down on virtually a frog pond, after fighting our way through many rapids and past so many bigger lakes.

We were at the mouth of a creek, and half a mile from a prominent hill, about 300 feet high. Our only exercise, and an alternative to lying huddled in a sleeping bag for warmth, was climbing this hill, which we did two or three times a day. We came to know the area pretty well, for we were camped in that spot for six whole days. Later we had the consolation of knowing that it was an exceptional and widespread blow, which grounded or docked all the HBC's planes and small craft, delayed their supply-boat, and deterred even the Inuit from going on the water. Uppermost in our minds now was the hope of reasonably prompt rescue, before we ate up all our supplies. We were carrying, as usual, a week's supply of emergency rations. Of greater concern was the question of how any plane or craft could even get to us, so long as the gale blew.

We had made the usual arrangement with the airline from which we had chartered, that if the pilot should find that we had failed to make the rendezvous, at the point where the Kazan entered Baker Lake on Chesterfield Inlet, he was to wait half a day and then overfly our route in reverse, and he would know from the written schedule which we had left him roughly where to expect to find us. We had always made such an arrangement, but this was the first time that it looked as though we should need it.

The days crept by. Even if the wind did eventually slacken, it would be impossible for any but the strongest members of the party to get to the mouth of the Kazan in time for our rendezvous, and even so, they would first have a long stretch into the north to contend with. Besides, splitting up the party would not achieve much. And by now there was not much point in our all starting off down the Kazan, even if we could, for we should certainly need a plane pick-up at some stage, and this little lake, much as we disliked it, would provide a better landing for the plane than would the fast river. For the present, anyway, the high wind made any move out of the question. We had a flash of hope on the second day, when a small plane flew low above us, but then disappointingly disappeared over the hill, evidently making for a very small lake on the other side. We debated walking over to talk to its pilot, but before anyone could start off the plane was up and away again.

Tom, whom we suspected of being a secret pyromaniac, was given the task of building a bonfire, to be lit when we heard our rescue plane. He achieved a monster pile of willow branches, carefully shielded from the northern blast by a canoe on its side, and with a tarpaulin over it to keep off the occasional snow-flurry. 'Has anyone thought,' enquired Peter one day, 'just how much per day we are each paying for this alleged holiday?' Pat made daily forays over the tundra, usually returning with a handful of assorted mushrooms and puffballs. 'There are no poisonous fungi in the Arctic,' he confidently assured us when we looked doubtful, so we ate them dutifully, only some months later learning that his information was not completely correct. One morning, when Pam and I had decided to let the others sleep in on yet another miserable day, we were greeted at 8 am by a cheerful little song at our tent door, and there were three of them bringing us breakfast in bed, bless their hearts. The wind was blowing so hard, and the tent flapping so much, that we had not heard a thing.

The day scheduled for our rendezvous came − and went. The pilots among us, Bill and Angus, were not surprised that there was no plane. We all kept an eye on that nick on the northern horizon through which the plane must fly, remembering how easily we had missed spotting the advance party on the Dubawnt, and wondering whether we could light the signal-fire in time in the gale. We felt sure we would hear the plane coming, for it would have to follow the river, and we were downwind.

In the event, we did not hear the plane at all, and our first warning was a call from Bill, who wisely had posted himself much of the time with his binoculars trained on that spot on the skyline. We sprang into action; every minute indeed counted, for the pilot was flying on a route up the middle of the lake, which was a mile or two from us. Frantically we tried to get the fire to light, but in vain, and the plane was drawing level with us. At the last minute, someone in desperation pulled the protecting canoe away to give more draught, and the flames and smoke leapt up. Dramatically, at the last moment the plane turned toward us, and landed on the lake, a few feet out from shore.

We learned then by what a narrow margin we had made contact, for the pilot had no more than ten minutes' fuel left before he would have had to turn back to Baker Lake and hand over to Search and Rescue the responsibility for finding us. For the same reason, he could not fly us direct to Churchill, as originally planned, but would have to take us to Baker Lake post, whence we could fly south next day. We had already realized that he would be unable to fly our canoes to Baker Lake, so instead we would have to stake them down at this lonely, windswept spot on the Barrens and have an Inuit later come out from the Baker Lake post by skidoo and tow them over the snowy tundra back to the HBC, where we had engaged to leave them at the end of the trip. It seemed the final twist of the dagger to have to leave our canoes to suffer such an indignity.

Inevitably, during our long pin-down and later, we reflected on what we could have done to avoid being foiled of finishing the Kazan. There had been occasions when we had elected to wait for better conditions, which did not materialize, and occasions when we seemed to have time enough in hand to have the luxury of drying out and resting. But this was hindsight, and they seemed good decisions at the time. One cannot, perhaps, expect to win them all. Nor does one really expect such a long run of poor weather and tough conditions. In retrospect, we do not remember the trip with ecstasy. And yet, even among the memories of the long days of discomfort and pin-down, there remain recollections of hours of good running on strong northern rivers, rapids that were challenging and fun, and days of dazzling sun among the ice-floes.

64 yrs. old
on this trip

Encounters on the Taltson

684 yrs old

When we came to decide where to make a trip in 1972, the Taltson River looked good. Guy Blanchet and Charles Camsell had explored parts of the river in the twenties, but there was neither record nor report of anyone having gone down the whole river since. In the event, the Taltson gave us a bonus of unexpected wildlife interest, for we witnessed in those three weeks a whole series of biological oddities.

The Taltson rises in barren highlands, with other large rivers such as the Dubawnt and the Thelon. It empties into Great Slave Lake near the delta of the Slave River, having followed a course roughly parallel with that lake's main axis. The river is about five hundred miles long, but at the Twin Gorges dam it is only thirty-five miles over to Fort Smith on the Slave River, so we chose to shorten our course to about 350 miles and fly out from the dam – a very short plane charter. On our way in, we first flew to Uranium City, and chartered a Twin Otter and a Beaver there, which would take our whole party of six, plus our gear and three Grumman canoes.

This time Angus, Pam, and I were accompanied by three 'youngsters' in their late twenties or early thirties: John Bayly, Terk's elder son; John Davis, who offered to be known as Johnny to avoid confusion; and his old school friend, Jim Matthews. The two Johns had been part of the crew I had recruited in 1970 to make a commemorative retracing by canoe, sponsored by the NWT government, of Franklin's route from Yellowknife to Coppermine. Despite the rigours of that trip, they were keen for more northern canoeing. All three were good athletes; John and Jim were both lawyers, and Johnny was at that time a stockbroker but soon after became bursar of the Pearson College of the Pacific.

Angus had earned a rest from being assistant cook, and he longed for more time to fish, so we set up a different arrangement which worked well. Each of the three youngest – John, Johnny, and Jim – would take a turn as cook's helper for a week. Jim, a bachelor, took his responsibilities so seriously that he had persuaded his mother to give him lessons in bannock-making before we set off. The two Johns justifiably felt that they had received plenty of training on their 1970 trip. I gather that the chief cook of that expedition, 'Hoop' Birkett, had his kitchen-hands so well subjugated that he would direct breakfast operations from his tent, snug in his sleeping-bag. Apparently he also had high standards of performance.

It had been twenty years since we had first started making our three-week trips in the west and north, and we had learned a lot in terms of equipment. Sig Olson had first introduced us to the splendid Duluth packs, capacious yet easy to pack into the canoe; easy, also – if that is an appropriate word – to double-pack, for one 60-lb Duluth pack can be swung up to sit solidly on the top of another. I had been fortunate in persuading an Ottawa firm to make near-copies of these packs, and these were in fact improvements. The canvas was not so heavy and therefore was easier to dry out, and nylon straps and ring-fasteners replaced the heavy leather straps and metal buckles, so awkward to wrestle with in the cold.

Lashing the packs into the canoe becomes especially important on remote rivers, where loss of gear could be disastrous. Lashing-in with ropes becomes so tedious when portages are frequent that there is a temptation to cut corners. To simplify the task I had stout webbing straps made, with strong metal spring-fasteners. It takes only a moment to slip one of these through the back-straps of two packs and round a thwart.

Our horrendous experience with blackflies on the Hanbury impelled us to seal every gap in our clothing. Velcro, fairly novel in the early sixties, provided the solution — we got the idea from a Stratford stage-designer who had to achieve a rippable shirt for each night's performance. Not only were the gaps above the cuffs of our shirts sealed with sewn-on Velcro strips, but we also had twill Velcro-bordered panels to stick over the front panels of our shirts on bad days, covering buttonholes and all. With the addition of elasticated cuffs for wrists and ankles, we could at least keep the blackflies from crawling inside our clothing.

Velcro

No longer were we required to obtain the document from the commissioner of the Northwest Territories which went by the grandiloquent title of a Scientists and Explorers Licence. The licence had always made us feel very grand and authentic; we noted that it expired on December 31 on each year, as if we had needed any incentive to get out by that time! My files remind me that in those years when the licence was required we were asked to supply the names and ages of all members of the party, together with a résumé of their canoeing and outdoor experience, also a statement of what equipment, food supplies, and clothing we would be carrying. It was emphasized that we were not entitled to shoot or hunt without special permission. And finally, 'some idea of when and where to look for you.' Fair enough.

In the kitchen department, Pam had made cutlery hold-alls of blue denim, modelled on roll-up tool-bags and with separate pockets for spoons, knives, etc. This made it easy to check after each wash-up, and avoid losses. Another of her innovations was to use rectangular baking-trays, instead of frying-pans, on long trips. Although they had to be watched carefully on the fire, because of a tendency towards burning, they were light-weight, stacked easily, and made more efficient use of limited fireplace space. It is, besides, much easier to cook fish in a rectangular pan than in a round one.

We had built up, over the years, our supply of plastic bags, jars, and waterproof stuff-bags. Plastic bags are important, for grocery supplies have to be removed from their cumbersome boxes and frail bags, and every ounce of food has to be carefully guarded and waterproofed. Ordinary plastic bags sold for household use are too thin, even with the additional protection of an outer bag of proofed nylon, but if the plastic bag is too thick it becomes brittle in the cold, and splits. Each canoe-party has its own way of organizing and packing the provisions. Many prefer to work out all their menus in detail, and to package each meal in advance. We never did this, for various reasons, one being that in tough conditions five meals a day may be called for, whereas on hot, easy-going days no-one may be very hungry. We found it better to arrange that there were enough breakfasts, lunches, dinners, and snacks for the whole trip, plus a week's emergency, and to leave it to the cooks to make the day-to-day decisions.

Food for such trips had gone through an interesting cycle. As far as possible, we would order our ordinary groceries through the HBC, but we were of course dependent also on lightweight foods, which had to be specially procured. In the early days of my travels with the Voyageurs, freeze-dried foods were not marketed in Canada, but the Defence Research Board was doing considerable research on their packaging and storing, having engaged specialists from the U.K. (where much of the development had been done). We were fortunate, through Omond Solandt, to be able to serve as a field-testing team; filing consumer reports was a surcharge we were happy to pay. And in those days the product was exceptionally good – only best-quality meat and vegetables for the armed forces!

By the early sixties, the franchise had been passed to a couple of Canadian firms, one of which soon dropped out. The other, run initially by ex-DRB staff, became our standby, but we sometimes wondered how long this would last, for the market was so small. Before long, the quality fell from its earlier pinnacle, and prices soared. The product was still acceptable, but we had been spoiled. Soon the explosion of interest in outdoor sport

such as mountain-climbing and recreational canoeing in remote regions of Canada increased the demand for lightweight
foods, and there were many North American suppliers to
choose from, and a bewildering variety of dishes. These days one
can stock up in freeze-dried foods from many well-equipped
sports stores: for us it used to be a protracted operation, taking
weeks if not months.

But not only had the quality suffered: the packaging had become less convenient for our purposes. The lightweight but
durable cans, frowned on by park authorities, had been replaced
by plastic or foil packages. I accept the reasons for the change,
but however strong the soft-pack it increased the risk of spoil-
age. Also it had become more difficult to obtain basic elements of a dish: the market was principally directed towards
ready-made 'complete' meals, with a few small nuggets of
meat buried in a mass of potato or pasta, which is a very expen-
sive way of obtaining those items.

Before the advent of freeze-dried foods, there had always been
air-dried foods, not quite so appetizing perhaps, but cheaper
and dependable. They suffered something of an eclipse with the
advent of freeze-dried foods, but I have the impression that
they are experiencing a come-back. And nowadays air-drying at
home has become an option, although adequate packaging
remains a hazard.

Other items became more difficult to obtain over the years.
There used to be excellent compressed meat bars, available
from England and from the U.S. Did they disappear because of
inspection regulations, or labelling rules, or tariffs? I have no
idea. Danish canned bacon, heavy in the packs but a delicious
treat when the slab bacon was used up, became rare. And no
longer could one be sure to find, in northern stores, those basic
supplies of the old hands, prospectors, trappers, and surveyors
– the cans of butter and shortening and wonderful big cans of
jam. Indeed, with increased air communication, the HBC
stores in the far north had become much like southern super-
markets. Progress of course, and presumably in the general
good, but we could not suppress a certain nostalgia.

Our food repackaging completed at Uranium City, we headed for
Coventry Lake, which appeared to be the source lake of the
Taltson River. I was sitting beside the pilot of the leading plane.
As we circled Coventry Lake before landing, I was dismayed
by the look of its outrun down a rocky rapid, into Dymond Lake.
The water was far too shallow and rocky for good rapid running, and there would be many more rapids on our route. If this
rapid was at all typical, we should be in trouble. However, a
quick check of the map covering the whole basin of the river was
reassuring, for there appeared to be enough tributary streams
to provide a good flow of water all the rest of the way. We avoided only the outrun of Coventry Lake, and put down on Dymond Lake, selecting for our first campsite a small island which
offered enough for our one-night stay. We dubbed it 'Camp
Adequate', and had our special first-night dinner of grilled steaks
and wine (wine being precluded for the rest of the trip, for its
weight).

The next morning we set out, entering at once our first set of
rapids. One attractive feature that had drawn us to this river
was its consistent drop. There would be two impoundments in
our total course, but the map indicated that they would not
rob us of much good rapid running. The weather all that first day
was delightful, sunny and breezy, and we had an exhilarating
run down several rapids, with no portaging, to a good campsite
high up on the bank. Here we were just passing the only small
stretch of Barrens we would encounter, and the view from the
hill beside the camp was unobstructed and spectacular.

It had been a good start, but we woke next day to rain and a
cold wind. Stubbornly, we set out, creeping along in the lee of
the shore, but in a mile or two the river changed direction,
broadening into a lake, and progress was impossible. We
walked, or huddled and read, while the squalls grew in intensity,
laced with snow. Finally, realizing that a cold front was coming through, we had to admit defeat, and retreated to the only
good campsite we had seen, that of the previous night, where
we dived into sleeping-bags and tried unsuccessfully to keep
warm. At times the snow obliterated the opposite shore. By

alcohol

dinner-time there were faint signs of improvement, a hot meal
helped, and the cure was completed by a bottle of Courvoisier.
I had secreted it in my pack, against the worst night of the trip,
and this seemed to be it. The glow from the brandy, a clearing
sky, and a spectacular rainbow sent us to bed in a spirit of
optimism.

We were on our way soon after six next morning, the weather
still cold, but the wind now from behind. The lake that had
turned us back the day before was really a shallow widening of
the river, flanked by an esker which jutted sand-bars into the
water along our course. There was ample evidence of caribou
and wolves, the beaches strewn with antlers and bones, and
the water's edge bordered with white winter caribou hair, shed
in every water-crossing. Keen to make up for the early pin-
down, we did thirty miles that day through shallow lakes and
several interesting rapids, cheered by the eventual emergence
of the sun. Our brief contact with the Barrens gave way to trees
again. Already we were getting the flavour of the Taltson,
characterized by the many sandy eskers and beaches which I
believe have something to do with its name. Almost all the
way, the campsites were park-like, shaded by small groves of
spruce and birch, with some jackpine.

McArthur Lake gave us a tough time, its shallowness causing
it to whip up sharp waves in the strong wind. All three canoes
were shipping water, and we camped part way along the lake,
hoping for better conditions next day, but the next morning
brought more of the same, and we had to battle on. The rapids
beyond were complex and fun to negotiate, requiring a mixture of lining and running; they would have been pleasanter
without the strong headwind. As we were working our way
down one long stretch of bouldery rapids, we thought we caught
a glimpse of something bright red ahead, and when we came
through to a lake, tired and ready to camp early at the fine campsite before us, there to our surprise was a single red canoe
drawn up, with two young men camping. They were as astonished
to see us as we them. There was plenty of space for our two
parties to camp together there, without disturbing each other.

They were brothers, from Seattle, and had been flown in the same day as we, but a little lower down. With a canvas Chestnut canoe, and little experience of white water, they were not attempting to run the rapids, and were taking their time. The fact that they had only made four miles that day did not bother them. Daylen, the elder of the two, was an interesting fellow. He was fascinated by the north, had read all he could about it, and was in the habit of quitting, every summer, his job in a lumber mill, and taking off in his canoe. He had picked the Taltson in much the same way as I had, seeking a river with the right characteristics by studying the map. In fact he had canoed the lower part of the Taltson the previous summer, with his wife and two small children, and had found it so much to his liking that he had returned to do the upper part with his brother. At Nonacho Lake, further down, a charter plane was to bring in his wife and children, and to take the younger brother, Randy, out. We questioned him about conditions lower down the Taltson, and it seemed there was nothing particularly threatening. Rather engagingly, he did ask us to watch out for one thing: a beaver dam (he described its location), where his children had stuck some poles and would be looking to find them again this year. If we saw them would we please not disturb the poles – the children would be disappointed. Somewhat to our surprise, when we reached the beaver dam we found that the beaver had left the poles untouched, and we were happy for the children. Such things can be very important at that age.

Strong wind prevented us from travelling at all next day, but we were able to set off early the following morning, and soon found ourselves in more rapids, most of which we ran, though we had some lining, and two or three portages. An amusing incident occurred at one rapid: Pam and I were in the lead and we were lining the canoe down most of the rapid, checking its speed and guiding it through the tangle of rocks near shore. I was on the stern rope and, at one fast elbow in the rapid, found the force of the current too great to continue lining, for the canoe was in danger of shipping water and foundering if we contin-

ued walking as slowly as we had to on the slippery rocks. I felt
that the canoe should be released, to run free, and called to
Pam to throw her bow line into the canoe, but she could not
quite hear me for the noise of the rapid. By the time she understood my frantic hand-signals, it had become too late for me
to do anything but cast off the stern rope first, hoping she
would follow suit, which she did, aghast. It was a risk, but
seemed the only course. With everyone in the party watching, holding their breath and fearing loss or wetting of our entire cargo,
the canoe, now free, shuddered for a moment and then took
off down the rapid, which it negotiated flawlessly, as if by remote control, all the bends right down to the lake at its foot.
There an eddy caught it and turned it back to the landing spot,
where it waited for us to get in. A roar of laughter went up,
mostly triggered by relief. But I noticed that none of the rest
risked the same trick. We had pushed our luck far enough.

The next day brought more rapids, long stretches of rocky
intricacies often with only a marginal course for the canoe to
run or line. At one, about half a mile long, we were astonished to
have spent about four hours on it, in our absorption not notic-
ing how the time was passing. We could have portaged it in a
fraction of the time, and agreed to do so in future if we were
behind schedule, but meanwhile all were enjoying themselves.

After this we entered a smoother stretch of the river, now
flowing swiftly between high sandy banks topped with spruce
and birch. We had the feeling of being in a zoo. There were bald
eagles overhead. Beaver swam around in broad daylight. Geese
and ducks were everywhere, the mother geese manoeuvring to
distract our attention and protect their young. One, so close to
the canoes that we could reach out and touch her, lay flat on the
water, neck stretched out and beak submerged, ostrich-like, as
if in some absurd way hoping we would not see her or would
mistake her for a rock or a log. A young moose, surprised by
our silent approach, crossed the river in front of us and tried to
scramble up the steep bank. Hooves scrabbling at the loose
footing, he panicked and turned, swimming back across the river
only just in front of the canoes. We came upon several other

moose, in ones and twos, feeding and apparently unconcerned about our presence. At the end of a small lake, there were caribou, only a few representatives of the huge numbers that evidently travelled through this area, on their winter migration from the Barrens into the woods.

A beautiful set of falls led us into Gray Lake, and we were blessed at last with tail winds on the next section of lakes. Our campsite partway down long, narrow Gray Lake was one that none of us will forget, an idyllic birch grove on a point, sunny, breezy, and bugless.

By now we were becoming aware that the water level was unnaturally high, and the shores further down were lined with drowned trees. Whole islands were under water, detectable only by the tops of the trees and bushes, and rapids had been drowned out. Evidently a dam had been put in further down since the map was made; we had in fact to interpret our maps in terms of this change in level. This became even more of a problem on the next lake, Nonacho, which is big and complex, the name meaning 'big points.' The course through the lake is tortuous, and the shoreline no longer conformed to the map. However, at one stage the high water and Angus' alert navigation saved us six or seven miles, for he had a hunch that an isthmus would be sufficiently inundated for us to paddle right over it. He was right, and we triumphantly named it 'Angus' Portage'. We were relieved when we came to the dam that had raised the level of Nonacho Lake, by five feet, and could portage around it to the natural level of the river again, free of dead trees and drowned shores. There seemed to be no power installation at the dam, so we concluded that the impoundment was not a primary source of hydro power but a storage area to maintain the flow for the lower dams during the heavy evaporation of hot summer days.

Here on Nonacho Lake, on a granite rock-face, we spotted some faint writing made long ago by scraping off the black lichen which covered the slab. We could just make out 'G.B. 1924.' Guy Blanchet, perhaps? It was around that time that he was on the Taltson.

Rapid on the Taltson River (Photo Angus Scott, Toronto)

By now a crisis had hit one canoe-team. Jim Matthews suffers from hay fever, and the pine-tree pollen had been causing him trouble all the way. After exhausting his supply of handkerchiefs and tissues, he had turned to toilet paper, and had finally run through all his own and that of his partner, Johnny Davis. The crisis had been hastened by the fact that both of them were rather lavish in their use of this important commodity. The rest of us put on a show of heartlessness in their plight, charging them with profligacy. Toilet paper became precious currency, to be bartered for. A plea for help from John Bayly, portaging a canoe, to get a blackfly out of his eye, was answered by Jim only at the price of ten sheets of toilet paper. Hard bargaining was the order of the day, but neither Jim nor Johnny could bring themselves to barter away their evening daiquiris, though there were several offers.

The Taltson here forms a chain of long narrow lakes. We passed into very long Taltson Lake, and saw the smoke of a forest fire for some distance, until the wind changed. The lake narrowed down to almost a canyon with a waterfall we should have to portage. Approaching the fall we saw a white wolf following us furtively along the shore. In the Arctic we had seen nothing but white wolves, which we concluded remained white year-round, the better to stalk their prey. Now we were in forest, where any wolves we had seen were brown or black. The white wolf left us, but unhurriedly. It was after all not very far from the Barren Grounds and may have followed the caribou down into the woods in winter time.

After portaging and lining past the rapids, we found ourselves on another long lake, King Lake, down which we had to fight a squally headwind, and were glad to find a sheltered campsite near its end. Jim had caught an 8 lb pike, which we poached and adorned with Hollandaise sauce, a memorable meal. As we were sipping our drinks before dinner, behold another oddity of nature. There in a small bay not far from us was a flock of loons – we counted at least fifty – massed on the water, possibly seeking the relative shelter from the strong wind. The strangeness was not just the size of the flock, but the fact that

it was made up of three different species. We identified representatives of all three species of the region – common, arctic, and
red-throated. Since the territorial imperative did not relate to
our present situation there was no calling, just a carpet of
bobbing loons in silent congregation.

The river which we were back into by now suddenly took a
hairpin turn and then led into a rapid with a right-angled turn
halfway down where the current was quite fast. We studied it,
debating the safest way to run it. There was a little bay, a nick
in the right shore, at the elbow. We decided the best way to slow
ourselves around the elbow was to run the first part, back-
paddle into the little bay, then come out from the bay and let the
fast current pick up the canoe and take it round the elbow.
The manoeuvre worked out as planned, one canoe after the
other coming down in picture-book style.

The rapid had been a pleasant surprise, for it was not marked
on the map. Now we were on another long, narrow lake, Lady
Grey Lake, and were immediately hit by a strong, almost gale-
force wind from behind, making it difficult to steer. We were
reluctant to be blown so far down the lake that we would have to
turn a right-angle and take the wind on our beam, so we gradually worked over toward the left-hand shore, where we found a
low flat point to camp, under the shelter of a small hill.

The lake drew in to river size and again we had another spell of
rapid running. Some of the map's 'rapids' were in fact ledges or
small falls, which had to be portaged. The river was dropping
fast, and the scenery was superb. At one rapid, Johnny and
Jim, who were ahead, made confidently for the slick of smooth
water, only at the last minute realizing that they were on the
lip of a ledge. Some frantic paddling enabled them to spin round
and reach a small eddy, just in time to escape disaster.

We had had some strange encounters, but now came one of
the strangest of all. As we were crossing a small lake below
Benna Thai Lake, we looked back to see a swimming moose
followed by what we took to be a moose calf. We turned and
paddled towards them, whereupon the smaller animal wheeled
round and made for the shore. There was something un-

mooselike about it, and as it scrambled up the bank and shook itself, we saw to our astonishment that it was a large wolf. It must have chased the moose, which appeared to be a young bull, into the water. I had never heard or read of a wolf taking to water to pursue its quarry. The moose saw us coming, three canoes abreast, but it seemed to regard us at first as its protectors, for it came on toward us, and only when we paddled our canoes alongside did it make for the shore and charge out of the water, splashing great white waves and offering splendid photography. The wolf meanwhile decided that its prey had too many friends in the locality and made off, stopping briefly to look back and perhaps curse us.

After some more rapids and falls, we came to where the Tazin River flows through a canyon to join the Taltson, and at the junction we identified a campsite described by Camsell, on a beach opposite the Tazin's inflow. This in fact is where he entered the Taltson, to explore its lower reaches. Here we decided to take a morning to look over the surrounding country. We paddled about half a mile up the gorge, then parked the canoes and climbed the steep hill before the start of the canyon wall. We were about 200 feet up from the river, and had a splendid view up and down both the Taltson and also the canyon of the Tazin. According to Camsell's account, the Tazin was in his day about the same size as the Taltson, but now it was only about half the size. The hydro developers had dammed Tazin Lake as a power source for Uranium City, letting most of the Tazin water flow directly into Lake Athabasca instead of continuing in its old channel down to join the Taltson. This had the effect, too, of reducing the flow in the Taltson below the junction, and we had shallow rapids to run as we approached our next waterfall.

That evening, at our campsite just before Napie Falls, I made a ceremonial presentation to Johnny. Our only smoker, he had run out of cigarettes a few days earlier. We always carry a supply of tobacco and 'the fixings', as well as tea, to have on hand to offer any locals who are particularly helpful or who seem to expect a handout. But now I explained that we considered

Pause for a snack and fishing on the Taltson

Johnny, with his withdrawal symptoms, to be more of a threat than angry natives, so he had better have the cigarettes. His joy and relief were almost comical.

Our next major rapid was the Three Bears, where we landed and camped at the top, so as to take them on fresh in the morning. First we broke into two parties, one to scout a possible portage, and the other to scout the rapids. The first of the 'bears' gave us a fine run down to the second one, past which we found ourselves on the lip of a low fall, with drowned land below it. We had in fact come to the head of the inundation caused by the Twin Gorges dam, where we were to take out to fly to Fort Smith. The rest of the way down to the dam was strange and rather depressing. We found ourselves floating over the tops of drowned trees, which had not been cleared out before the flooding. Although the scenery had now lost its beauty, and we could easily have gone on to Twin Gorges, we preferred to have our last night in camp, so set up our tents on a point about three miles from the dam. Johnny, Jim, and John paddled on after lunch to phone our charter airline and make a rendezvous for next morning at the power house.

After the shortest charter flight that we ever took, we found ourselves at Fort Smith, delivered our rented canoes to the Hudson's Bay Company, and spent the afternoon sight-seeing the historic Fitzgerald Portage on the Slave River, with a pleasant cocktail party with friends before boarding our plane for Toronto.

The Taltson River had been a delight almost all the way, even better than we had expected. Few rivers can offer such a succession of pleasurable rapids, through such exquisite country. In all the 350 miles or so, we had no more than four or five miles of portaging, mostly short and easy. Disadvantages are the two stretches of inundation, the land uncleared before flooding; to some, the string of long narrow lakes would be a deterrent. Our own special rewards were the feeling we had of being the first to canoe its upper reaches for several decades, and the astonishing sights of birds and animals that we had encountered. In fact, it was such enchanting country that we made a pact, perhaps selfishly, not to publicize it lest it become spoilt. But now a number of people have found it, and the secret is out.

Across the Mountains

Canoeing over the continental cordillera was perhaps the biggest challenge of all, greater than crossing the Barren Lands. For anyone wishing to go any farther west than the high mountains flanking the Mackenzie, stretching from the American border all the way north to the Arctic Ocean, this 1500-mile wall had to be surmounted at some point. The CPR, going through the Rockies, had chosen to cross the continental divide at an altitude of about 6000 feet, and the Peace River canoe route used by Mackenzie in 1793 achieved the crossing at a similar altitude. By comparison, the route which passed via the Rat River from the Mackenzie delta through McDougall Pass crossed the Richardson Mountains at an altitude of only 1040 feet. It was scenically attractive, even though it meant abandoning almost all thought of paddling on the way up. Robert Service went over this route, as also did Stefansson, and many of the Klondike gold-seekers, starting from Edmonton. To this extent the route played its slim part in the Canadian story of the opening of the West.

It would, of course, be hard work going up the Rat River, but this was countered by the fast rivers, the Bell and the even faster Porcupine, coming down from the summit. I had long had a hankering to see this route, and in 1965 I organized a party to make the trip. I had been keen, too, to paddle the 3000 miles

from Hudson Bay to the Bering Sea, and this would be the key
to getting through the mountains.

The party was six: Terk Bayly, Pam, and I, together with Bill
Sheppard, Jack Goering, and David Woods. David was the jun-
ior member in age, and also the least experienced as a canoeist.
He made up for this handicap by his keenness. He was an
Australian, meeting not only a new sport but new country, even
for Canadians. Both he and Jack were masters at Trinity Col-
lege School and Bill, on the bench of the County and District
Court, Toronto, was a frequent canoe-racing companion of
Terk's. Our craft were three 17-foot Grumman aluminum
canoes.

To start this 600-mile trip, we flew first to Inuvik, planning
thence a charter flight to Fort Macpherson, at the foot of the
mountains and just south of the Mackenzie delta. Fort Macpherson is one of the most northerly of the Hudson's Bay Company's posts on the mainland. The furs that it feeds into the
HBC international trading corporation are trapped mainly by
the Loucheux Indians living at Old Crow on the Porcupine.

At the float-plane base near Inuvik, Shell Lake, where we were
to pick up our charter flight, we had bad news: our advance
baggage had not arrived. The arrangements for its shipment had
been made months earlier, in meticulous detail, and we had
had confirmation that it had reached Edmonton more than a
week ago. Either it had been forgotten, or the company responsible for bringing it on to Inuvik had cut things too fine.
This had the makings of a major disaster, for the shipment
included most of our cooking equipment, all the freeze-dried
food and other food items not available at Inuvik, and some of
our tents and sleeping-bags. The thought of trying to replace all
this, at short notice, in Inuvik was a nightmare. The radio
operator in the flight shack was optimistic, telling us that there
was a plane on its way up, and with a bit of luck it might have
our gear on board. We persuaded him to keep trying to make
contact with the pilot, but reception was terrible. Eventually
he announced that he *thought* the pilot said that he *thought* he
might have the baggage on board, and with this we had to be

content. Our charter pilot went off on another mission, while we spent the time checking the supplies that had been ordered from Inuvik, and then cooked our first-night steaks on a make-shift grill fashioned from rusty wire, eating everything with our fingers. To the astonishment of the pessimists among us, the plane from Edmonton did in fact have our belongings, and our charter pilot came back for us.

We arrived at Fort Macpherson in the early evening. Alerted by Inuvik to our late arrival, the HBC factor at Macpherson had kindly kept open for us, so that we could pick up our rented canoes and purchase a few remaining supplies. Terk stocked up with some cigars which had the double effect of driving away the bugs and everyone else from his vicinity. He later admitted that the factor had given them to him, having been unable to sell them. The Indian children at Macpherson were hugely interested in the process of repacking the groceries in water-proofed bags, and all wanted to help. Decanting the overproof rum from bottles into plastic flagons was even more of a sensation. Finally we had everything packed, and we camped on high ground not far from the trading post, looking down from a high embankment onto the Peel River as it rushed to join the Mackenzie delta. Here it was, since we were now within the Arctic Circle, that I had my first view of the midnight sun hanging just above the northern horizon.

The mosquitoes in that delta area were around us in clouds. We thought we had become inured to northern bugs, but these were something else. The operation of relieving oneself became minor torture, and we wished we had brought some spray-cans of repellent to ward off the intrusion at these intimate moments.

We did not hurry unduly to get away next morning. The first day always requires more time to break camp, and the only accounts we had had from predecessors on the route gave us confidence that we could easily reach the site of the Klondikers' Destruction City, where the route starts to climb up to the pass, in six hours' paddling. (How wrong we were!) We managed to get away by 10 am and headed straight north, down the Peel River. Though it was a warm day for that latitude, we

were to be reminded again, almost at once, that we were inside
the Arctic Circle, for we found to our dismay that wherever
we wished to land, for whatever purpose, the ground was only
just starting to emerge from deep winter frost. Every bit of
bare earth, not protected by vegetation from the direct rays of
the sun, was a sea of sticky mud, like a spread of melted chocolate, two or three inches deep. We hoped for cool weather, since
our whole route to Alaska would be within the Arctic Circle.
Camping, unless on rock would be a problem. That day there
were to be many more problems than that for, in sum, we
paddled on from 10 am right through the Arctic half-light till 5
am next day before finding a place where the bank was dry
enough to land and camp.

I should explain at the start that the Rat River, probably in a
spring flood, had split at some time in the past into two outlets, virtually making a north Rat and a south Rat both flowing
into the Husky Channel of the Mackenzie delta. What was
particularly discouraging was that the air photographs on which
our map had been based must have been taken at a time prior
to the split, though we had no difficulty in identifying the Husky Channel, nor where the south Rat entered just a mile down
it. Only much later did we realize that what our predecessors on
this route had evidently done, and what we should have done,
was to hire an Indian with a strong outboard motor to take us
twenty miles farther down the fast Husky Channel and then
up the north Rat to Destruction City, this being a much shorter
and less tortuous course than the south Rat. We had been
misinformed at Fort Macpherson.

Another signal of the state of the terrain greeted us as we
started up what our map called the Rat River. There was a
continual 'plopping' sound from the high mud banks, and at first
we thought this came from muskrats alarmed by our approach, diving into the water. Soon we realized that the noise
was from lumps of melting mud dropping from the unstable
banks. This sound accompanied us most of the way to the summit, and the resulting murkiness of the water made fishing un-
rewarding and the rocks difficult to see.

The river twisted and turned interminably between high mud banks, our navigators painstakingly tracing our position all the while on the map. Their diligence at one point saved us three miles of paddling by hauling the canoes across the base of a big loop, up the bank and down the other side, a matter of only fifty feet. The afternoon wore on; at a teatime break we made the astonishing and depressing calculation that at this rate we could not reach Destruction City before midnight. Worse was to come. Suddenly, fifteen miles up the Rat, the navigators found that the map no longer conformed to the river. We had not passed any fork: clearly the unstable river had in its overflow changed course since the map was made. There had already been other evidence of the shifting conditions in this area, for when we entered the Rat, the fallen trees which festooned the banks, undercut at their roots, pointed upstream, not down. We concluded that the channel we were on, with its sluggish current, served as an overflow outlet for the Peel (flowing in the opposite direction) during the spring flood. The alluvial banks, whip-sawed by strong currents, must be constantly apt to change.

Now virtually without a map, we pushed on grimly, for we had to reach firm ground before we could camp. We were nearing the foot of the mountains, which we could glimpse from time to time, but now our channel passed through an area of small lakes and ponds, where the current was scarcely detectable, and we often had to spend time probing for the true exit to a pond. In such a spot we had our evening meal, perched uncomfortably on fallen tree-trunks just above the water. Then it was back to more winding, upstream paddling, through the dusk of an Arctic night.

Sometime after 3 am, we joined what was quite obviously another channel, and found ourselves paddling against a much greater volume of water. We were at last on the Rat proper, and we even welcomed the effort of fighting the stronger current. In about an hour, we sighted the first piece of bedrock on shore, another cheering sign. And round a bend was our goal – a spread of flat, dry turf where it would be possible to camp.

Four people at a time were sometimes needed to haul a canoe
up the Rat River.

This was undoubtedly the Klondikers' 'Destruction City', the point in their journey where they knew that they would have to abandon their boats and get ready to contend with snow in the mountains. The first rocky riffles were just ahead. Here it was that they knocked down the boats in which they had floated down the Mackenzie and worked up the Rat. This was the reason for the word 'Destruction'. With the boards, they made sleighs which they had to drag to the summit and then convert back to boats, so as to float down the fast Porcupine to the Yukon River.

Before setting up camp, and despite the indecent hour, we felt we should celebrate having reached Destruction City through such uncanoeable country. So, at five am, we made daiquiris and dug into a large jar of caviar brought by Terk – in contrast to the grim conditions suffered by those of the Klondikers who had wintered there.

Our first task next day was to cut ten-foot poles and shoe them with the metal ferrules which we had brought. We were faced now with getting up a shallow rocky river, virtually a continuous rapid, for forty-five miles to the pass, climbing at an average of twenty-two feet to the mile. There would be little hope of paddling until nearly the top – only a succession of lining, poling, and sometimes plain manhauling. We made the first rocky riffle by poling. But soon after that we came to a steeper part, where the river was boiling over boulders with great waves, and sterner measures were needed. The only way to overcome such a current was to put four people to a canoe, manhauling it, then 'park' that canoe and go back for the next.

We had realized from the start that we should have our legs in the water for most of the time from now on. The river was constantly braiding, twisting and turning. At every bend, the stream had to be crossed to reach the inside of the curve, where the current was slacker, the river-bottom firmer, and the shore more likely to provide a beach for tracking. Usually we would wade across, clinging to the canoe and sometimes to a crew-mate's belt. If it was too deep to wade across, or the current too strong to keep one's footing, we would get into the canoe and paddle over in a cross-ferry, angling the craft to the current. The howls of our predecessors, in their journals, on the subject of the low temperature of the water – especially in the upper sections, near the pass – had got through to us. We had accordingly provided ourselves with both long johns and the lowers of 'dry' suits. These, plus thick socks, kept the body so hot that the cold water was almost necessary for comfort. The only uncomfortable chore this entailed was putting on, each morning, those wet, cold garments, worse than a wet bathing suit.

Our speed was working out to be only five miles a day. We had hoped to better this, but were beset by another problem: a day of rain caused the river to rise two feet in the night, increasing the strength of the current, robbing us of lining beaches, and forcing us in places even to pull our canoes up by clutching branches along the shore. Like many river basins in this latitude, with few trees and with permafrost so close to the surface, the valley of the Rat does not sponge up water as do river valleys in more forested, warmer regions. Rain quickly produces a flood. But by lining, wading, and poling we did make progress, through grim persistence. The varied means of moving the canoe did give rest to certain muscles, although after three days or so we found that our toes were taking a beating. They were bruised and blackened by the constant battering of underwater rocks. Our canvas running shoes, chosen for wading, gave little protection, and though new were themselves wrecked in a week.

Soon after this we experienced what could have been a fatal disaster. We had all warned David on no account, when pulling up rapids, to tie himself to the canoe. However, while no one noticed, he had adopted this seemingly sensible way to pull against the increased current, and just before where a tree jutted out at a particularly steep drop in the river, he had tied the painter around his waist and started to climb over the obstruction, about six feet high. The canoe went out of control and he was whisked off his feet. Luckily he, or the rope, caught a root as he hit the water and the rope broke, leaving the canoe

Shoes wore out

to hurtle downstream, for Bill had been unable to hold it on his own. Terk and Pam, who were about a quarter of a mile ahead, happened to be looking back and caught the dramatic sight of David flying through the air into the water. They tossed their packs on shore, leapt into their own canoe, and raced downriver, shooting three rapids before they came upon Bill and David. These two had somehow contrived to run some way along the tree-cluttered bank, but had then attempted to wade across the river after the canoe and had been swept off their feet. They had managed to swim to shallow water, and piled in with Pam and Terk for a ferry to where the runaway canoe could be seen a little further downstream, overturned and grounded on a shoal.

The canoe had suffered only minor damage and was repaired without trouble; the packs, which had been lashed in, were of course soaked. Most of the contents were waterproofed, but a few bags of flour and rice had burst and were wet. The toilet-paper was a write-off. We were lucky that the results of the accident had not been worse. When we reviewed events, it emerged that the rope had been noticed that morning as being frayed, but replacement had been delayed. Perhaps this was fortunate, in these circumstances, but we noted that it was dangerous in principle, and that we should inspect our ropes carefully each day.

Next morning we had a stroke of luck. Every day of our journey up the Rat we had been gazed at from above by a helicopter crew, heading to a point over the flanking hills. This day they landed at our camp, evidently suspicious of us and wondering what we were up to. They were working for an oil company, with a base-camp nearby, and were delighted to find that we were not in rivalry. When they asked if they could do anything for us, we were able to tell them of our recent calamity and our spoiled provisions. They insisted on our making a shopping list for them, saying they would return in a day or so. When they did return, it was to give us only one item from the list, which had particularly impressed them and which they had singled out for high priority, namely toilet paper, of which they

Using a combination of tracking and poling near the top of the
McDougall Pass

had brought eight rolls to replace just the two that we lacked! However, they did kindly bring us some luxuries: eggs, orange juice, and real coffee. One disquieting piece of information that they gave us was that their prospectors were all armed and were in the habit of shooting at any grizzly bears they saw, of which there were several. We felt alarmed to think we should be travelling a course where wounded bears were likely to be roaming.

Just before reaching the 'First Canyon' on the Rat, we identified where, in the winter of 1931–32, Albert Johnson, the 'Mad Trapper', had holed up in a cabin and defied a combined force of white trappers, Indians, and an RCMP detachment. Johnson wounded two of the Mounties and killed a third, a corporal.

Working up the river really demanded all one's attention, but when we could lift our eyes and gaze around us, the scenery was spectacular, the mountains lying back some distance from the river. Progress was so slow that a prominent feature of the landscape would be there for days, seemingly impossible to pass. Curiously, there have been several reports of people losing their way up the Rat, although navigation is not that difficult. An early party took a tributary, the Barrier River, a mistake that modern maps would make unlikely. Further on, at the Forks, three creeks join to form the Rat River, and here the correct course is the middle one, Rat Creek. Even as recently as 1983, we heard of a German party taking the wrong turn, perhaps at this point.

The bald, snow-streaked Richardson Mountains had been edging closer, but now we lost sight of them as we entered a tunnel of trees, up the brawling Rat Creek. Again we had to put four to manhauling each canoe. Soon, near the top, we came out on a more peaceful scene, where the creek winds through a mountain meadow, the water deep enough and the bottom firm enough to make for good poling. We had reached an altitude now where we could see the peaks at the summit, along the height of the Richardson Mountains. It was truly scenic with barren peaks rising 4000 feet above us. The ridge itself marks the boundary between the Northwest Territories and the Yukon

and is, of course, the continental divide. The sky was blue overhead, but each mountain peak had its own small cloud of
cumulus, where the warm Pacific air was being pushed up into a
colder altitude and condensed, revealing the reason for the
rain forest on slopes rising from the Pacific Ocean. To reach the
final, half-mile portage over the divide, all we had to do was to
pass through a few small lakes, with only one quarter-mile carry
to the last pond.

At the end of this pond, before portaging over to Summit Lake,
we looked back down the way we had come. Here was an
appropriate spot for our evening meal. It was truly an occasion to
celebrate, for we had attained the summit, and had no more
climbing. Two-Ocean Creek, well-named, tumbled down a short
distance away, feeding water both into the Rat on one side and
into Summit Lake, draining into the Pacific, on the other. For
the last time the canoes were hauled out of the waters of the
Rat, and we sat down to a festive meal of whatever special goodies we could find to eat, with a bottle of wine specially
brought for the occasion, followed by liqueurs. We even, with
that view, tolerated Terk's cigar, though no one accepted his
offer to share his supply.

Dishes done, we felt rested and refreshed to tackle the short
portage over the pass. It is notable that only this single half-
mile portage separates the two vast basins of the Mackenzie and
the Yukon rivers, which together drain over 100,000 square
miles.

An attractive campsite lay before us on a turf-covered knoll
by the shore of Summit Lake, with a gorgeous view of the
peaks of the stark, treeless Richardsons rising about us. For the
first time in several days we had an unobstructed view in all
directions. We had originally planned to have two or three days
at this spot, exploring on foot the mountains at the summit,
but the rise in water-level following the rain had put us behind
schedule, we estimated, by four days. Side trips on foot would
have to be abandoned.

So instead, we set off next day to paddle the half-mile length of
Summit Lake, finding at the other end that beavers had raised

a four-foot dam of willow branches and mud to block the outlet of the lake westward. The solution of course was to break the dam, but before doing so, we felt it would be prudent to make a short reconnaissance ahead. We found below the beaver dam only a very small flow of water, also dense willow branches that had grown out from the banks making a low tunnel over the watercourse. With the increased flow gained by breaking the dam, the tunnel roof would be too low to permit paddling, and if we raised the water too much, even the canoes would not get through. What we decided to do was to work quickly destroy-ing the dam – quickly, so as not to lose too soon the head of water we needed to float through on – and then, as the dam broke, to leap into our canoes, crouching low so as to have as little obstruction as possible above gunwale level, and to let the flow of water carry us without attempting to paddle. For the half mile of the outlet creek this worked, and got us to the Little Bell River, leading into the Bell, a tributary of the Porcupine.

It was a joy to be travelling downstream again. The Little Bell presented us with a few runnable riffles and rapids, though we had to wade and line a few, finding the mountain water icy cold without our dry suits, which we had thought we would no longer need and had abandoned. Winding our way past towering cliffs and pillars of rock, we came before long to the Bell River.

Now we were in different country altogether, and also a differ-ent climate. The air was moister and rain-showers were not infrequent. The river became wide and fast, sweeping in ever-greater curves between high banks of alluvial soil, where tall trees leaned out or lay fallen. Campsites were less easy to find, and we often had to settle for a small gravel beach wherever we could find one, usually at the point where a small tributary entered.

Halfway down the Bell, we came to Lapierre House, built of logs and still standing. We spent a little time going through its rooms; it looked to have been abandoned about fifty years be-fore. Lapierre House in fur trade days was an entrepôt having the same function as Grand Portage and Norway House. The

furs of the Liard basin were abundant and of good quality
because of the cold. However, the Liard River, in its lower
reaches approaching the Mackenzie River, had a bad reputation
with voyageurs, for its canyons, its murderous rapids, and its
brutal portages. Accordingly, this direct route to the Mackenzie was forsaken for a more circuitous route, from Lake Frances
down the Pelly River and the Yukon, to Fort Yukon, and thence
up the Porcupine. At Lapierre House the 90-pound portaging
loads of furs were repackaged into smaller backpacking loads,
so that they could be carried on a mountain trail, flanking the
Peel River, down to Fort Macpherson near the Mackenzie delta,
whence they made their way to York Factory and shipment
overseas. There had been some thought among us that the site
would provide a good place to camp, and we had pushed on
longer than usual in order to reach it that night, but it turned
out to be a jungle of tall weeds, almost the height of the house,
and in the hot windless evening the bugs were legion. We
resigned ourselves to paddling on.

As we swept in from the Bell to the Porcupine, we came upon
an Indian and a white man in a motor-boat, from Old Crow,
who had come up to cut trees for building. We floated along
beside them. I was talking with the Indian, Charlie Abel, who
first informed us that by the 'bush telegraph' the RCMP at Old
Crow had already had word that we would be four days behind
schedule. Possibly the oil company crew we had met had passed
on the word. I remarked to Charlie Abel, 'I guess you think
we're crazy spending our summer vacation like this,' to which
he replied, 'No, if I lived Outside, I think I would want to
come to this country.' This was the chief of the Loucheux band
of Indians, based on Old Crow. The band's affluence was de-
rived from the trapping of muskrat in the Old Crow flats. They
possessed a relatively high standard of living and made head-
lines around the world when, in 1942, the band sent a substantial donation for the relief of bombed-out victims of air raids
in Britain.

We stayed with the Porcupine all the way to where it flowed
into the Yukon River. It was a fast river and we found our-

selves able to make sixty and sixty-five miles a day (as compared with five, coming up the Rat). The only problem in navigation was to read the water constantly to ensure that we remained in the fast current and did not get caught in an eddy or stranded on a gravel bar. Occasionally a canoe did jolt to a stop on a shoal, obliging its crew to step out into the shallow water and spend time and effort pulling the canoe through, or more usually pulling it back and working over to a better course.

The scenery, now we had left the high mountains, became monotonous, for the river flowed through large-sized spruce, which grew right down to the water. When we came close to the bank, we had to watch out for the occasional 'sweeper' below the surface. However, we were making good time. Now and again at lunch, instead of landing, we would lash our three canoes together, assign one person to look after steering, and picnic in the canoes. Serious thought was given to the possibility of saving even more time by using the same technique to travel at night, but eventually we decided that the risk, in the half-light, of running up on a gravel bar was too great, and the idea was abandoned.

About a mile from Old Crow, we passed a solitary cabin, high on the bank. It was time to get ourselves spruced up, in the tradition of the voyageurs when coming to a settlement. While we were drifting and burrowing in the packs for clean clothes, we heard a shout. The Indian owner of the cabin, one Ken Negum, had helpfully put out in his canoe to warn us that we were not on the best approach channel: the current would wash us up on a sand bar, and he pointed to where we should go. We watched in amazement as he negotiated the swift current, for he had only one arm, and paddled with the paddle shaft tucked into his armpit. Almost his first question to us had been an anxious 'Have you seen the caribou?' We gathered that they were late that year, and that the village was accordingly deprived of meat.

We were amazed at Old Crow to be greeted at the dock by microphones thrust at us, and people asking us about our journey. It so happened that a CBC crew had flown in that day to gather material for a special broadcast on the community, and various members of the press were on hand to write up the CBC's story. In my search for suitable clothing to wear coming into Old Crow, I had found a sweater with the name of my old school, TCS, emblazoned on it. I didn't think this bit of advertising, in the distant wilderness north of the Arctic Circle, would be unseemly. However, to my amusement, as I landed a tall reporter from the *Edmonton Journal* greeted me with outstretched hand, announcing, 'I'm a Pickering man myself.'

The RCMP corporal in charge was relieved to see us, for no less than three expeditions coming up the Rat had got lost in recent years. He had a telegram for us, received from a friend of ours who was officer commanding the RCMP Arctic Division. But instead of reading to us just the message of congratulations, he handed me the whole telex from headquarters, which started, ominously, 'If Eric Morse and party complete their trip successfully as far as Old Crow, please hand him the following message ... '

We had at Old Crow a rather touching example of the fabled hospitality of the North. Normally, when we receive such hospitality, we think that we have not much to give in return except the contact with the outside world and any world news we can bring. But in Old Crow, an Indian woman had come while none of us was around and deposited in our drawn up canoe a loaf of freshly baked bread. We didn't even have a chance to thank her. Interestingly, too, a distinction was made between ourselves who had travelled there the hard way, and the 'city slickers' of the CBC who had flown in. Whereas we were entertained for supper by the RCMP and were presented with other gifts of food by Indians in the village, we heard the CBC ask sadly, as they sat waiting for the one little store to open, 'Where's all this northern hospitality we hear so much about?' We paid the obligatory visit to the village celebrity, Miss Edith Josie, as she liked to be titled. It was partly the fame of her weekly column in the *Edmonton Journal* that had brought the CBC to Old Crow. Next week, in her 'Letter from Old Crow' in the *Journal* she noted: 'Evening three canoe arrived Old Crow.

They are Morse party ... . Sure long way they travel to see Old Crow how it look.'

A sequel to this encounter with the CBC was that after we returned home they asked us to appear on a national TV interview on 'Take Thirty'. When we met at the studio in Toronto, the leader of the field crew said to Pam, 'What I remember most about you is how dirty your hands were' – memories of the Snare! This seems to be the fate of all kitchen staff on canoe trips. Tony Lovink, one of our crew on earlier canoe trips, had to dine at the Netherlands palace just after returning from one of our Voyageur trips, on which he had done the scrubbing of pots. As the senior diplomat of the Netherlands, he was seated beside the queen, and had to keep his hands well hidden throughout the meal.

Still four days behind schedule, we decided to make up some of this lost time by hiring an Indian and his motor-powered freighter canoe (at only $1 per mile) to take us sixty miles on our way. This boat took us, in the Arctic dusk, from Old Crow down to Old Rampart House, on the Alaska border. The river through the canyon, on the way there, is fast and can be rough when, as sometimes happens, a south-west wind blows up the valley. Our boatman told of once being windbound there for three days even with his thirty-foot boat and outboard motor. We were fortunate to have got through this with no strong wind to oppose us.

At Old Rampart House, the buildings had long been abandoned. We needed shelter, for the boat ride had been horrendous. The cold of the mountains, especially in that latitude, the wind created by our speed of travel, the lack of any roof or shelter, and the fact that we were no longer paddling combined to make the sixty-mile ride a very frigid experience. The two who had travelled below deck, lying on the thin planks against the chilly water, were even more uncomfortable.

We stopped on a small island opposite Old Rampart House, to build a fire, brew some hot chocolate, and have a snack. It was about midnight, and semi-dark, but our Indian boatmen headed back right afterwards, and we set up camp. At our campsites just

Floating lunch on the Porcupine River, the three canoes lashed
together and making good speed

before Old Crow, we had come to realize the coldness of air
mattresses set on ground where the permafrost was so close
below the surface, and knowing that we had still a few more
nights to camp in this latitude and altitude, we had managed in
Old Crow to purchase six roughly-tanned caribou skins to put
below our air mattresses. This made a world of difference, for
the caribou, like any deer, have hollow hairs as insulation.
Next morning we took time to look at the old buildings, across
the river, then went on – now in Alaska.

From here on, the river braids often, and we had to be alert, in
that fast water, to pick a channel that would take us all the
way through without grounding. Since the water was still high,
some of the smaller channels were navigable and acted as
shortcuts. It was important, too, to detect the fast-moving 'river
within a river', seldom the shortest route but usually the
quickest, snaking from side to side between the eddies. The
helmsman skilled in analysing the 'grain' of the river surface
and picking up this magic carpet was rewarded by effortlessly
outdistancing those of his toiling companions who had not
acquired the knack.

In due course we approached the junction of the Porcupine
with the Yukon River. Fort Yukon lies on the Yukon, two
miles above this junction, and we knew from reports that it
would be difficult if not impossible to ascend the swift Yukon
above the junction, the river being too deep for poling, and its
banks too high for lining. The alternatives are to arrange a tow
by motor-boat up those two miles of the Yukon, or to portage
over from the Porcupine without going down to the junction.
We chose to portage, so our canoeing ended there where we
camped, on Homebrew Island on the Porcupine River. Next
day we would start wending our way back by various air-hops,
from Fort Yukon to Fairbanks, Whitehorse, Edmonton and
home, leaving our U-paddle canoes to be towed up the Yukon to
Dawson City, the nearest Hudson Bay post.

When I saw the Yukon River, its breadth and muddy water
reminding me of the Saskatchewan or the Mackenzie, I lost
any further wish to follow it down to the Bering Sea. Moreover,

it would involve at the end paddling on the open sea; and communications to arrange a homeward flight would be difficult.

In short, Fort Yukon was the end of the trip, the 'end of the line'. In fact, the end of the saga. We had reached the limit of good water flowing westward. And also the end of the westward route of our historic predecessors, the Klondikers, who at Fort Yukon turned eastward up – not down – the Yukon here to reach their goal, the Klondike River.

Coming back to civilization after a trip in the wilderness is always something of a sadness, a 'splashdown' from another world. This time the return trip was unduly protracted, partly because we had to recross a continent, but also because of bad connections. Scheduled flights in the north seem to have a tendency to arrive at a staging point just half an hour *after* the only plane that day, for the next point, has left. Perhaps the intention is to generate hotel business; it does have the merit of breaking one in gradually to people, noise, and all the things that have become unfamiliar. But subconsciously, a part of oneself is still back in the wilderness. At our Whitehorse hotel, the first night off the river, Pam in her sleep was obviously still coming down the Porcupine. In the middle of the night, she woke me with an urgent cry, 'Quick! We're running onto a gravel-bar!' Not quite awake enough to protest, I got up and looked out the window. Nothing was there but the main street of Whitehorse. The only gravel in sight was not under water but on the roadway. The hotel was on a safe course!

Envoi

As I look back over the memories of a lifetime of wilderness canoeing, the rewards far outweigh the rigours and discomforts. In fact a catalogue of the rewards seems hardly necessary. Spectacular mountain scenery was a prime reward of our journey through the Richardsons, between the Mackenzie and the Yukon rivers. To this could be added the grandeur of Lake Superior's north shore; the less awesome, quiet beauty of the pine-clad, smooth rocky islands at the mouth of the French River and along Georgian Bay's north shore; the joy of running a rapid on a big river like the Coppermine; the silence and solitude of travel in the Barren Lands; the many exciting encounters with wildlife that such travel brings; the sense of history in the early journals we carried, sharing the excitement and experiences of the explorers and traders who had preceded us; the delight of living an outdoor life and stretching oneself to the limit; the camaraderie of the trail, with the right crew, chosen for their skill, stamina, and compatibility – these all add up to something perhaps best described as 'out of this world.'

Index

Maps

The features in the maps on the following pages have been
selected to illustrate particular journeys; features unnecessary for this purpose have been omitted. Besides the routes
which have been described in the book, other canoe-trips I
have made which happen to fall within the areas covered by
the maps have also been indicated. The starting and finishing points are all shown by year.

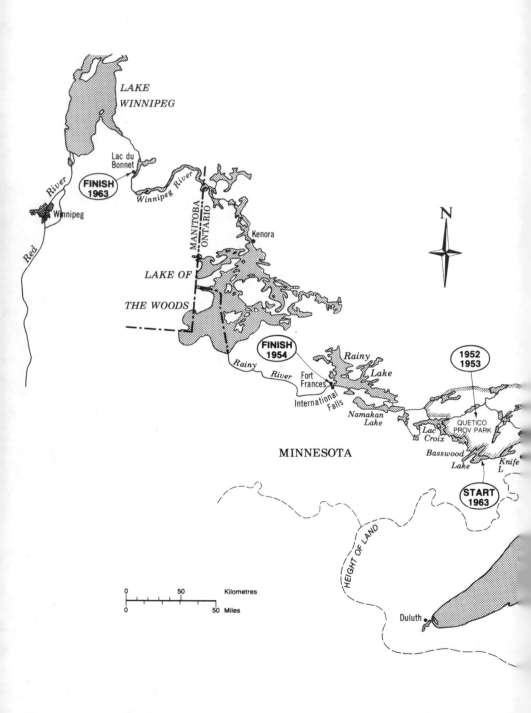

LAKE
WINNIPEG

Lac du
Bonnet

FINISH
1963

Winnipeg River

River

MANITOBA
ONTARIO

Winnipeg

Red

Kenora

LAKE OF

THE WOODS

FINISH
1954

Rainy

Rainy

River

Lake

1952
1953

Fort
Frances

International
Falls

Namakan
Lake

QUETICO
PROV PARK

Lac
la Croix

MINNESOTA

Basswood
Lake

Knife
L

START
1963

HEIGHT OF LAND

N

0   50   Kilometres
0   50 Miles

Duluth

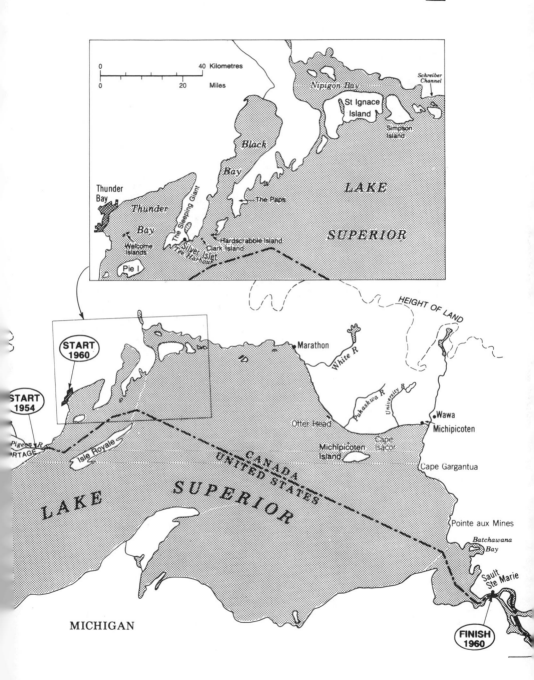

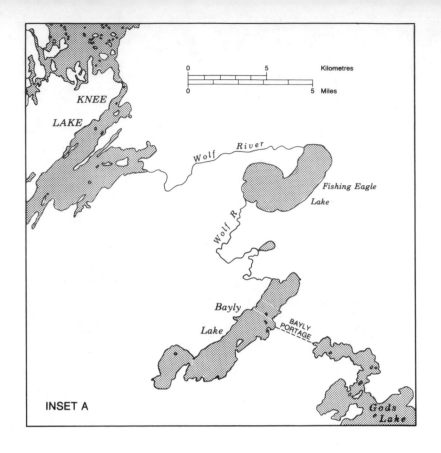

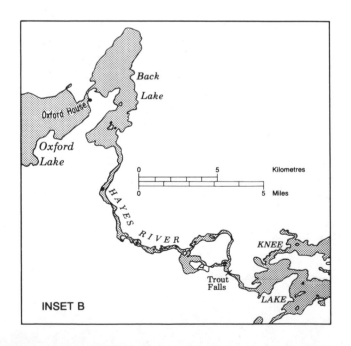

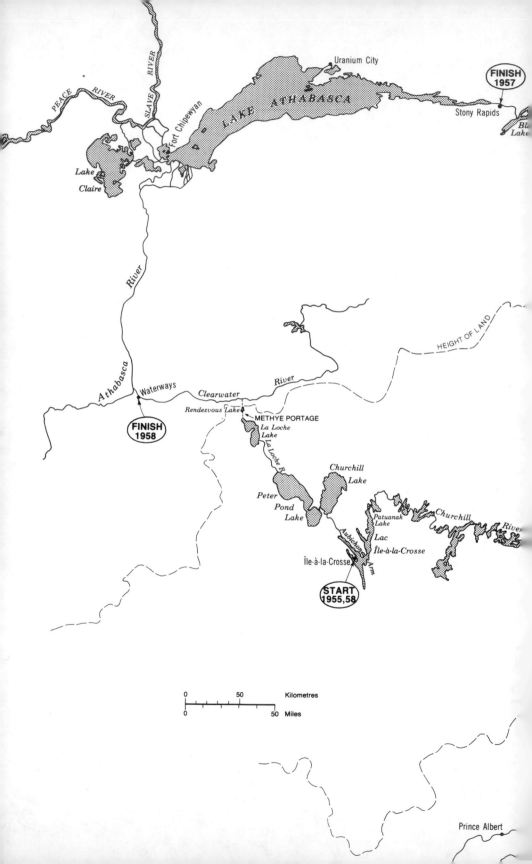

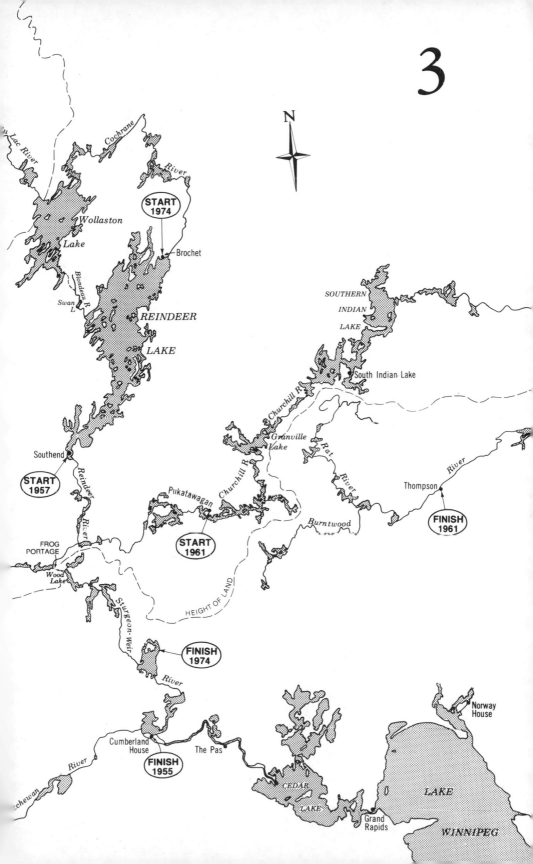

3

N

START
1974

Cochrane

River

w Lac River

Wollaston
Lake

Blondeau R.

Swan
L.

REINDEER

LAKE

Brochet

SOUTHERN

INDIAN

LAKE

South Indian Lake

Churchill R.

Granville
Lake

Churchill R.

Rat

River

River

Thompson

FINISH
1961

Southend

START
1957

Reindeer

River

Pukatawagan

START
1961

Burntwood

FROG
PORTAGE

Wood
Lake

Sturgeon-Weir

HEIGHT OF LAND

FINISH
1974

River

Norway
House

Cumberland
House

The Pas

River

FINISH
1955

chewan

River

CEDAR

LAKE

LAKE

Grand
Rapids

WINNIPEG

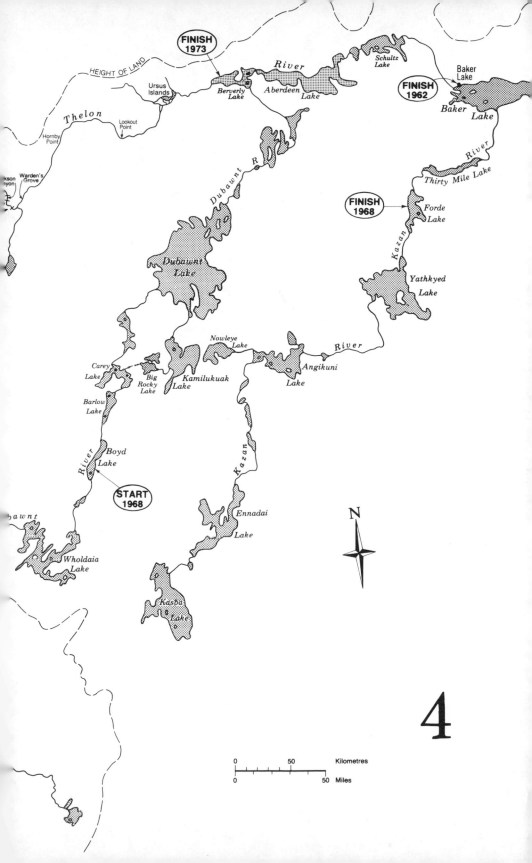

FINISH
1973

HEIGHT OF LAND

River

Schultz
Lake

Baker
Lake

FINISH
1962

Ursus
Islands

*Beverly
Lake*

Aberdeen   Lake

*Baker
Lake*

Thelon

Lookout
Point

Hornby
Point

River

kson
nyon

Warden's
Grove

Dubawnt R.

Thirty Mile Lake

FINISH
1968

*Forde
Lake*

Kazan

*Dubawnt
Lake*

*Yathkyed
Lake*

*Nowleye
Lake*

River

*Angikuni
Lake*

Carey
Lake

*Big
Rocky
Lake*

*Kamilukuak
Lake*

*Barlow
Lake*

River

*Boyd
Lake*

Kazan

START
1968

*Ennadai
Lake*

N

bawnt

*Wholdaia
Lake*

*Kasba
Lake*

4

0   50   Kilometres

0   50 Miles

HEIGHT OF LAND

GREAT BEAR
LAKE

Port Rad

FINISH
1959

Norman Wells

Mount
St Charles
Bear

Fort Franklin

Great

River

Fort Norman

MACKENZIE

Camse

RIVER

N

MACKENZIE

LIARD RIVER

RIVER

Coppermine
loody Falls ✕

**FINISH
1966**

5

Coppermine

River

HEIGHT OF LAND

Point Lake

**START
1966**

Lac de
Gras

Winter
Lake

Aylmer
Lake

Tranakoie
Narrows

Roundrock
Lake

Indin
Lake

Snare
Lake

Snare

River

Jolly
Lake

Courageous
Lake

Snake R

Outram
Lakes

Lockhart River

Clinton
Colden
Lake

MacKay
Lake

**START
1964**

Snare

River

**ART
59

Bigspruce
Lake

Dam ✕

Slemon
Lake

Artillery
Lake

River

Fort Reliance

Lockhart River

Rae

**FINISH
1964**

Yellowknife

Snowdrift

GREAT SLAVE
LAKE

Taltson
River

Fort Resolution

SLAVE RIVER

0   50   Kilometres
0   50 Miles

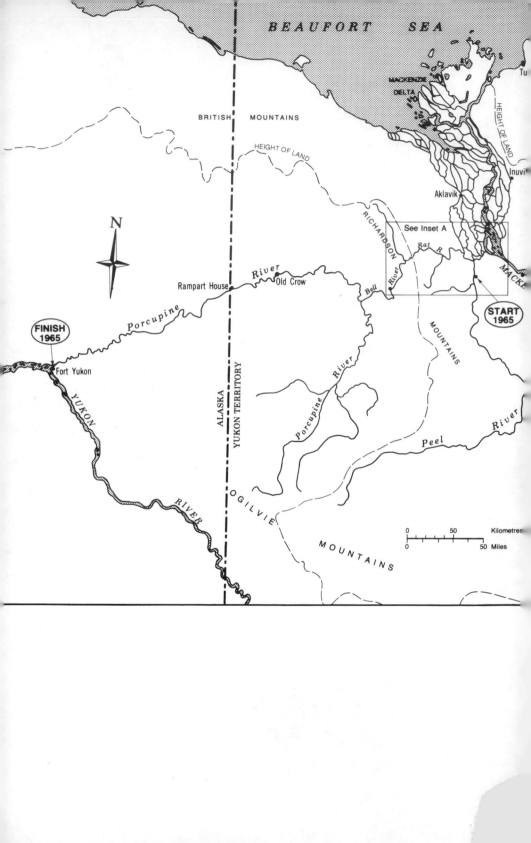